Cornerstones and Core Needs
of
Growing Kids

Life Is Full of Choices Series

life is full of choices

John Emra

www.LifeIsFullOfChoices.org

Creative Team Publishing

Creative Team Publishing
San Diego

© 2011 by John Emra.

All rights reserved. No part of this book may be reproduced, stored in a retrieval system or transmitted in any form or by any means without the prior written permission of the publisher, except by a reviewer who may quote brief passages in a review distributed through electronic media, or printed in a newspaper, magazine or journal.

Permissions and Credits in order of appearance:

Quotation from *The Scarred Heart: Understanding and Identifying Kids Who Kill* © 2000 by Dr. Helen Smith used by permission.
Quotation from Dan Wagner, Senior Homicide Prosecutor, Orange County, California used by permission.
Word definitions taken from *Merriam-Webster's Eleventh New Collegiate Dictionary*.
Scripture quotation marked (NLT) is taken from the Holy Bible, New Living Translation, copyright © 1996, 2004, 2007 by Tyndale House Foundation. Used by permission of Tyndale House Publishers, Inc., Carol Stream, Illinois 60188. All rights reserved.
Quotation from *Instinctive Parenting* by Ada Calhoun used by permission.
Quotation of purpose statement for Celebrate Kids, Inc., Kathy Koch, Ph.D., President and Founder used by permission.
Quotation from *The Vital Touch: How Intimate Contact With Your Baby Leads To Happier, Healthier Development* by Sharon Heller, Ph.D. used by permission.
Quotation from Dr. Jenn Berman, author of *SuperBaby: 12 Ways to Give Your Child a Head Start in the First 3 Years* used by permission.
Quotation from Robert MacKenzie, author *Setting Limits with Your Strong Willed Child* used by permission.

ISBN: 978-0-9838919-0-1
PUBLISHED BY CREATIVE TEAM PUBLISHING
www.CreativeTeamPublishing.com
San Diego

Printed in the United States of America

Cornerstones and Core Needs
of
Growing Kids

Life Is Full of Choices Series

life is full of choices

John Emra

www.LifeIsFullOfChoices.org

The Three Cornerstones

Cornerstone Number One — Empowerment
Life is full of choices,
and the choices I make today
will determine the qualities of my life
both now and in the future.

Cornerstone Number Two — Responsibility
Life is full of choices,
and the choices I make today
can affect the circumstances of my life
and other people's lives
both now and in the future.

Cornerstone Number Three — Freedom
Life is full of choices,
and even though I have not chosen
all the circumstances of my life,
I alone determine its qualities, because
life is full of choices,
and the choices I make today
will determine the qualities of my life
both now and in the future.

The Four Core Needs

Affection
Anything we do to make a child feel good
about him or herself.

Boundaries
The pre-arranged limits that are placed on behavior.

Consistency
Doing what you said you would do.

Discipline
The actions that are taken to instill in a child
the understanding of right and wrong
in order to shape their character
so they learn how to make healthy choices.

Table of Contents

Cornerstones   4

Core Needs   5

Foreword   9

Introduction: A Basketball and a Bag of Candy   11

1 We Didn't Know What We Were Doing   19

2 Cornerstone Number One — Empowerment   29

3 Mending Fences   49

4 Cornerstone Number Two — Responsibility   53

5 Rules and Results   65

6 Introducing the Four Core Needs   73

7 Affection   85

8 Boundaries   95

9 Consistency   107

10 Discipline   113

11 Cornerstone Number Three — Freedom   129

12 Choices or Decisions   137

13 When, Where, and How   145

14 Where Are They Now?   163

Conclusion and Acknowledgements   189

Life Is Full of Choices (www.LifeIsFullOfChoices.org) 193

Foreword

This is the story of John and Sheryl Emra and the work we began in 1986 at the Los Angeles Community Center in the Boyle Heights section of East Los Angeles. From 1986 through 2001 we regularly had more than 1,000 kids each year involved in one activity or another at this facility. We were busy!

We loved the work. We loved the kids, their families, and the growth we saw in them and ourselves. While we worked with kids from the community we raised our own children, too. Sheryl and I have two sons, Brian and Paul. I use their names when referring to them. I use the terms "children" and "kids" interchangeably when talking about the young people we chose to adopt into our hearts and lives at the Community Center.

We learned valuable life lessons from working with all of them! There were many exciting experiences and many that were tremendously disappointing. Growth occurred in every one. During the early years Sheryl and I worked together at the Community Center almost all of the time. We developed the programs, curriculum, and procedures while trying to figure out *how* to do what our sponsoring mission had sent us there to do.

This story is not about needing credit for any idea; rather, it's about the ideas we came up with and how they worked. We hope you gain important insights as we reveal what we learned and taught. Perhaps these ideas will work for you.

This is our story but it really is the story of what God did through us. His action generated what we came to call the Cornerstones and Core Needs of Growing Kids. We invite you to explore these with us and to learn how lives can be changed.

Introduction:
A Basketball and a Bag of Candy

Children don't come with instructions.

I was at the hospital when both my children were born — in fact I was in the delivery room for our second son's entry into the world so I know without a doubt that when he was delivered an instruction booklet was not taped to his bottom.

However, even though children don't come with instructions, parents do. Parents, we have an instruction booklet taped to the inside of our subconscious. That instruction booklet influences, if not forms how we raise our children. We either raise them in the ways we were taught and experienced, or we decide to follow alternate paths and raise our kids differently.

Sheryl and I were pretty fortunate with the instruction manual that was connected to our subconscious. We agreed on most of the methods we used to raise Brian and Paul. When we had differing ideas we were able to negotiate and choose a course of action we both wanted to follow.

We had moved to Los Angeles in 1986. Our mission organization had sent us with a mandate: to find a ministry that would affect the neighborhood for eternity's sake. As we surveyed our surroundings we saw 8,000 kids going to school within seven blocks of our front door. What we observed about the school system, however, was startling. The dropout rate for Junior High kids alone approached 50%. The drop out rate for High School students was another 50%, and *still* there were 8,000 kids going to school.

Overcrowded schools and overwhelmed teachers: that was a major problem. There simply wasn't a serious effort within the school district or the neighborhood dedicated to help these kids stay in school. Sheryl and I saw hundreds of kids just hanging around. Most of them had neither direction nor hope.

Our choice was simple. We put our energy into helping those kids in East Los Angeles. We started an after school program called the Los Angeles Community Center. We started the Center with a basketball and a bag of candy.

Our family showed up one day and started playing basketball in the Center's parking lot. As we played seven kids jumped over the wall and started playing with us. After an hour or so we sat down and told everyone a Bible story and gave them a piece of candy. We told them we would be back the next day. The following day we came back and so did they, and this time they brought some friends.

At that time Sheryl and I didn't know anything about inner city ministry. We knew even less about gangs and how they operated. But there we were and we chose to make a difference. That first month Sheryl and I began the "PhD Degree Program for Inner City Youth Ministry." It was taught to us by the kids in our neighborhood. It was an intensive course. The classes in which we were enrolled were conducted daily by the true experts in the field.

The lessons we learned developed into the cornerstones and core needs we describe in this book. For a while we didn't even realize that *we* were the learners. We were slow to grasp what was going on around us. While we were teaching them about God and the impact He could have on their lives, they were teaching us about living in the inner city.

Our main limitation was our reluctance to admit, even to ourselves, that we even had things to learn. Preconceived notions sometimes got in the way of acquiring the understanding and wisdom working with these kids offered.

Eventually we overcame that handicap. We became more teachable and we learned a lot from "our kids."

One of the first lessons we grasped was that the inner city is not a good place to raise children. Then we realized that the families of the children with whom we worked were not as fortunate as our own. Most parents of inner city kids didn't have a good instruction manual in their subconscious. Most of them were just trying to survive a very tough life in a most difficult setting.

Economic pressures often forced both parents to work outside the home. Combined with a poor educational system, hopelessness was the result. This dire situation created strong temptations to take any available shortcut to discover success. Often this shortcut meant joining a gang and that choice could overwhelm the hopes and dreams any parents may have had for their children.

Children want their parents to provide emotional, mental, physical, and spiritual guidance. Most kids want to grow up to be responsible adults. Helping kids achieve this success is simply part of the responsibility of raising them. For thousands of years children have grown up pretty well. Parents have worked hard to create a better life for their kids than the one their parents experienced.

Now, somehow, that system isn't working well anymore.

Parents may still work hard but it seems that kids, at least kids in the inner cities, are not responding to their parents' hard work. These kids are becoming more violent, more remote from society, and harder to communicate with.

Social media has consumed many of them. Pressures to conform come from gangs, movies, video games, and internet websites. Kids are influenced beyond their capability to understand right from wrong. Caught in the crossfire of overload these kids receive severe scrutiny and their actions do not lend themselves to positive interpretation.

Dr. Helen Smith in her book, *The Scarred Heart: Understanding and Identifying Kids Who Kill* says that "…kids appear to have no remorse and leave the rest of us confused and terrified. Violent teens are every parent and school's nightmare, if you believe what you read in the papers and hear on the news. We have all heard the horror stories of younger and younger kids who are picking up weapons and harming or killing others."

Search the internet for the phrase, "Kids are more violent." You may come up with what I did: more than *36 million* possible sites that deal with this topic. Expand your same internet search. Look for the topic "21st Century gangs" and you may find an even more impressive *47 million* web pages.

Evolving statistics tell us there are more than 30,000 gangs with more than a million gang members across the United States. With about 700,000 police actively deployed it is easy to see that the police are far outnumbered. Some commentators referencing gang organizations have compared them to the structures of terrorist organizations like Al Qaeda. Like a terrorist organization, the effects are alarming and frightening when a gang takes over a neighborhood.

In the mid 1980's there were few if any groups compiling national statistics about gang proliferation. For the most part, commentators were silent. The only people who seemed interested in gangs were the police and they were cautious.

Soon after moving to Los Angeles and opening the Community Center we discovered neighborhoods in the Los Angeles area where police do not travel alone and where they never respond to a call except in force. We discovered that the Center happened to be in one of those neighborhoods. In fact, the intersection on which the Community Center sat was claimed by four different gangs, one on each corner. We learned this fact one day when we called the police about a stolen car and eight squad cars arrived at our front door from four different directions at exactly the same moment.

We also learned that life in the inner city is impacted by societal systems that are broken. Three of them, the educational system, the justice system, and the emergency medical system are completely overwhelmed. This condition deeply affects the way our kids see themselves and the possibilities for their future.

Dan Wagner, Senior Homicide Prosecutor, Orange County, California commented, "For several years in my career in the district attorney's office, I worked as a prosecutor of juvenile offenders. In every juvenile offender case, a probation officer prepared a social history concerning the juvenile's family background and upbringing. Reading these reports on a daily basis, I was struck by an unmistakable reality: in almost every case, those youthful offenders had no responsible, caring adult role-model in their life. Not coincidentally, they had an impoverished sense of personal responsibility, no grasp on the consequences of their choices, and no vision for how they could shape their own future. If someone had been building into the lives of those juvenile offenders those kids would not have been breaking the law and getting locked up."

All of this composes a snapshot of the quicksand where Sheryl and I were living and working. It was an environment of virtually no foundations and no anchors.

As a family we traveled across the United States raising the needed funds to live and run the Community Center. During those trips I talked to hundreds of groups about the belief system we originated at the Center called, "Life Is Full of Choices." Following our presentations people would come up to us asking for more information. Two phrases that were constantly repeated were, "I need this for my kids at home…" and "I need this for my classroom."

I talked with scores of parents. I heard the stories of families struggling to raise good kids. Some succeeded, others failed. I was told about two siblings growing up in the same household. One child would make it all the way through school and become a positive member of society while the other would drop out of school and join a gang.

I heard tales from parents' perspectives. With tears in their eyes they talked about their immense frustrations. Many believed they were not doing a good job of raising their children. They didn't know what to do to make a positive difference.

I heard similar stories from teachers' perspectives. Kids were falling through the cracks in the educational system. The teachers who didn't like it couldn't change it. They were frustrated and angry because they saw their efforts to educate this generation producing mixed results at best.

This book tells the story of how we lived, how we learned from the kids who taught us, and how we chose to make a difference in the lives of our teachers. The lessons we learned and the principles we discovered apply in any life and all circumstances. Try them in yours.

1

We Didn't Know What We Were Doing

People often ask, "Where did you first get the idea of focusing on the choices that kids make?" Well, in the beginning Sheryl and I were just like a lot of parents. We had two young children and didn't quite know what we were doing.

Sheryl and I are missionaries. In 1980 we received our first assignment and relocated to Honduras. Our job was to work with the National Church. Our goal was to learn the language and customs of the Honduran people, and spend time with a National Pastor to learn how to live and work in a Latin Community. For two years we lived in La Esperanza, a small town in a mountain valley on the northwest side of the country.

Being missionaries in a country other than our own certainly introduced us to different lifestyles. We learned that to be effective we had to change our behaviors. Adapting new behaviors can be difficult, but for us the most challenging, dramatic, and lasting life change occurred in 1984 when my parents came to visit us on the mission field.

They had been with us for a couple weeks. One afternoon my dad and mom took us aside to talk with us about discipline. They had observed our pattern of parenting. One method we used was counting to three when we asked Brian, age six, and Paul, age four to do something and they didn't obey right away.

"Brian, don't do that! I'm going to count to three and if you don't stop that I'm going to be mad. One, two, two and a half, two and three quarters…"

My parents had heard those kinds of words over and over. Finally they decided to say something. They told us that counting was not necessarily bad but the way we were doing it simply gave Brian and Paul three extra seconds to continue doing whatever they were already doing. The point was this: If they could mind us by the count of three, they could mind us at the count of one.

My parents shared with us that we were establishing negative discipline patterns with our children. We were responsible for demonstrating examples of behaviors that would take our kids into adulthood. As adults Brian and Paul would use these models for the rest of their lives. What we were doing in the safety of our home would someday be used in the yard and the school playground. Later in life those patterns would be applied in the workplace and in interactions with other adults.

They said the problem with what we were doing would surface when we really needed them to respond to us *now*: that moment when the ball is rolling into the street and a car is coming and I yell to stop; that instance when Brian is moving to put the scissors into the electric outlet and I need him to respond to what I am saying right then. The car and the electrical current won't wait while we count to three.

At some point I remember saying, "That is too much. I don't want to have that kind of responsibility." My dad answered, "John, you already have the children. It is too late now to change that. At this point, whether you like it or not, you have the responsibility. From now on, you can only choose what patterns you are going to establish."

From that moment we started to understand the responsibility we had for shaping Brian and Paul's lives.

There were no options here. They were our kids, we loved them, and we had to be the ones to invest in them.

Fast forward a few years and we're living in Los Angeles. We had started the after school program in a rough neighborhood and were working with a small group of kids, helping them doing homework, involving them in recreation, and teaching them in Bible Club.

Bible Club was not just a casual activity. Like most missionaries, we wanted to see conversions. We would read scripture, tell a story, memorize a verse, and then ask for children to raise their hand if they wanted to accept Jesus into their heart. We wanted those raised hands. We wanted to count those hands. It is rewarding when a report is sent to your mission organization that includes large numbers. People get excited about those numbers. Supporters seem to be more motivated to give and pray when they read news letters that report large numbers of kids coming to Jesus.

Every week we were seeing growing numbers of raised hands. We felt this was good. And it was. But it wasn't good enough. The problem was that we weren't seeing many changed lives along with those decisions. Raising a hand was one thing; experiencing positive life change was quite another.

Our mission operated three inner city youth programs in California. We were in charge of one of them. About two years into our work in Los Angeles two other program leaders and I decided to join our efforts and hold a combined winter retreat at a camp in the mountains of central California.

I remember the trip to the camp, oh so well. That day of drama resembled a disturbing and unending nightmare. Sheryl and I drove an old fifteen-passenger van. We had that van packed so tightly with luggage, food, craft supplies, and sports equipment that I am not sure where we found space for thirteen kids. We drove eight hours through the California desert, then up narrow and winding mountain roads.

During this adventure Sheryl and I spent much of our time yelling at the kids.

"Don't do that!"

"Don't say that!"

"Keep your hands to yourself!"

"Leave her alone!"

"Didn't I just say, 'Keep your hands to yourself?'"

"Leave him alone!"

"Don't say that!"

"Would you *please* keep your hands to yourself?"

That day in the van we practiced an exercise of sheer futility. We said the same things over and over again hoping that somehow the kids would change their behaviors. But "Don't do that. Don't do that. Don't do that. Don't do that. Don't do that…" didn't work.

Looking back on that trip I am still amazed that we survived. But we did, and it was worth it.

We had arranged for a youth pastor from Ohio to be our guest speaker at the retreat. His topic for the weekend was, "What Choices Are You Making?" In his talks he described the choices kids make and the results of those choices. He stressed the important connections between choices and consequences. He made a strong impression on his audience, especially on me. His topic hit home. It made total sense. Frankly, I may have received more out of that weekend than the kids did.

At the end of the retreat there were some raised hands; but for me, the most important experience of the weekend was the trip home. I actually looked forward to it. I wanted to apply what I had learned about choices.

One of the more aggravating problems we had endured with the kids centered on the music they wanted to listen to while traveling. They wanted to choose the radio station so they could choose the music. We, on the other hand, didn't want them listening to songs that contained swear words or lyrics with sexual innuendo, elements usually hidden by loud volumes. We were constantly fighting with the kids because of these differences.

When we "won" and were listening to something we thought was appropriate, the kids complained and got into trouble. If we gave in and listened to what they wanted they behaved better but Sheryl and I were miserable because we knew the influence of the music was not good. As a result we spent a lot of time and energy listening for bad words. We were not pleased when we heard them.

On the trip home that weekend, I chose to make a few changes in the way we operated. The first change was that instead of Sheryl sitting next to me in the front seat, the kids got to choose who would ride shotgun. The main responsibility of whoever would be riding shotgun would be to decide which radio station we would listen to. Before we started the van I made it plain that Nathan, the kid who was voted to ride in the front, was in charge of selecting the radio station while I was in charge of the volume.

The kids thought this was a great deal. I think they were

focused on what they wanted to listen to without thinking it all the way through.

Five minutes down the road the song that was being played was obviously unacceptable. The kids were singing along and the lyrics were not good. So I reached over and turned the volume down so low that no one could hear the song. I didn't turn the radio off, just lowered the volume.

You would have thought someone suggested eating raw liver for dinner. Everyone screamed at Nathan to turn the radio back on. He was looking at the radio and saw it was still on. He was having trouble understanding why no sound was coming through the speakers.

When the kids settled down enough to hear me I explained that the radio was still functioning. I told them I had chosen to turn the volume down because the song being played was unacceptable.

It took a while for them to realize that the privilege of choosing the radio station carried the responsibility of making sure that the radio station was playing music acceptable to the controller of the volume—me. Over the next couple hours, learning occurred. Every time I turned the radio down the kids got better at working together to decide what they wanted to listen to.

There's a valuable lesson here. As long as I reacted *every* time I heard something unacceptable on the radio and followed though with managing the volume control as I promised I would, things went along pretty well. When I got distracted and let something slide by, chaos would result. Consistency of *my* behavior was not optional.

When I made a mistake I had to start over again and explain what I was doing and why. Then I had to deal with, "Why are you turning it down now, you didn't turn it down the last time?" and "That's not fair, that's my favorite song!"

Here's the bottom line: when I was consistent things went well. When I was inconsistent the system fell apart.

When the system worked the kids discovered that yelling and screaming didn't matter. They learned that if they wanted to enjoy the radio they had to make better choices about the station they wanted to listen to.

That day I recognized that if I—
Gave them the control of their actions,
Set clear boundaries about what was acceptable and unacceptable,
Told them what would happen if they crossed those boundaries, and
Followed through *every time* they stepped over the line, then I was not emotionally invested in the result.

I could react to their actions without yelling or getting mad. Their behavior had become their responsibility. They had just earned the consequences of their choices.

Sheryl and I discovered that it was possible for us to ride with them in the van for eight hours without fighting with them. In fact, after a while they started working *with* me. Instead of trying to see how much they could get away with some of the kids started thinking ahead about which radio station they should choose.

They started making better choices. Their improved choices made our driving time home much more enjoyable.

That was the beginning of a journey for me. I had discovered a tool I could use with these kids that would help me help them. We could interact in a better environment. We would survive our time with them; all of us would enjoy the experience more, and eventually relish building relationships that would last.

2
Cornerstone Number One — Empowerment

The trip home was an eye-opener. I had come to realize that a simple change in my vocabulary could empower the kids. My choice to change my behavior gave them the power to make better choices in their lives as long as my behavior was consistent.

Sheryl and I decided that our goal would be to take our after school program which was already having a positive impact on the lives of at-risk kids and give the curriculum a more focused approach. The goal became to not only reach more of these young people for Christ, but achieve lasting results beyond their conversions.

The kids around us didn't realize that life was made up of a series of choices. They didn't know how to make beneficial choices either for themselves or others. Further, they didn't want to accept responsibility for the outcomes of the choices they made. They were just living life as it came.

People make choices everyday often without thinking about the consequences. We wrestled with that reality. It caused us to seriously consider this question: How could we just let these kids go through life without showing them that the most important choice they would ever make was whether or not to build a relationship with God?

We knew that God wanted to have a relationship with them. God had made it possible to develop that relationship. We needed to make the possibility of that relationship a reality. Since everyone makes choices and all are judged by their choices, Sheryl and I wanted to help our kids make the best choices they could.

We believed that when kids understood the ramifications of their choices their understanding would make a huge difference in the ways they made their choices. We wanted to show them that life without an awareness of their choices would lead to hopelessness, defeatism, and fatalism and that not understanding consequences, would make life intolerable.

We wanted to teach our kids that whether a person consciously thinks about choosing, or unconsciously responds to stimuli and acts inadvertently, that individual is still going to be held responsible for their choices. Other people will hold them responsible and eventually God will, too. We wanted to make sure that our kids learned this vital truth: The choices that I make right now determine the qualities of my life.

The choices that I make right now determine the qualities of my life.

Weeks after the winter retreat we observed a growing trend at the Community Center. Kids started complaining that I was talking all the time about their choices.

One day as I arrived to open up the Community Center I noticed Maggie, one of our teen girls, sitting on our steps swearing at a boy who was walking by on the sidewalk. I didn't see what had happened to start this exchange between them. All I needed to know was that one of the rules we had on our property was, "No Swearing."

I stepped in front of Maggie, got her attention, and said to her, "What choice are you making?" She looked at me with a smirk and said "What difference does it make? I want to be at the Community Center today. Either you let me in, or not. I don't know what you're going do so it really doesn't matter to me."

Right then I knew there was more to learn. As I talked with the kids about their understanding of choices I discovered that they didn't think I was consistent in following through with a consequence. That realization initiated two changes in my life. One change occurred in my vocabulary and the other was a realization that consequences were important.

We had clearly experienced a correlation between choice and consequence in the van episode but at the Community Center the kids did not see the connection between the two. If they didn't see the connection at the Center they saw it even less in real life. Their conclusion became that while their choices might generate some kind of result, they couldn't predict what that result would be, so it wasn't worth worrying about.

It occurred to me that saying "Life is full of choices" had no power in the lives of our kids where they really lived. My vocabulary needed to shift. That statement had to be given more meaning. A framework for the statement had to be constructed so they could relate to those words. We had to make that sentence real.

Consequences lived in the consistency of my actions. My consistency in the van had affected their behavior and made the van ride home bearable for me. It wasn't just the choices the kids had made, but what happened when those choices had consequences!

Consequences lived in the consistency of my actions.

We decided to change our expression. We expanded the words we were using. Soon "Life is full of choices" read like this:

Life is full of choices,
and the choices I make today
will determine the qualities of my life
both now and in the future.

Sheryl and I understood this collection of words would be important to us. We wanted to give the words a meaningful name. We called it a *cornerstone*.

As we developed our ideas we knew these words would impact what we did at the Center and how we interacted with our kids. We understood that this Cornerstone would be the start of a foundation upon which the kids could build the structure of their lives.

We talked, discussed, argued, and sometimes even fought about the words we would choose to describe the cornerstone. We wanted to get it right, to communicate well how choices and consequences were connected.

The most important concept of this cornerstone was that it was expressed in the first person singular. It was "I." These are my choices, it's my life. These will be the qualities of my life, and they will frame my future.

> Every moment provides a choice waiting to be made and every action reveals a choice already made.

The moment a person of any age understands the ramifications of these words is the moment they take control of their life. They begin to see how choices are considered and made all day long. They realize that every moment provides a choice waiting to be made and that every action reveals a choice already made. Once that thought sinks in they have taken control of their lives. At that moment they are empowered!

We had come to realize a painful reality about our kids: they were steeped in a culture of fatalism. Their view of life could be summed up like this: "It doesn't matter what I do. I am going to end up just like my father, mother, brother, uncle, brother, or sister."

- "My brother is in a gang; therefore I will be in a gang."
- "My father dropped out of school so I will, too."
- "My sister got pregnant at sixteen, so I will probably end up pregnant."

Maggie was not embarrassed or upset about what she had done because she didn't know how I was going to react to her swearing. As a result she expressed no concern about what she felt she had no control over anyway. That was an illustration of fatalism.

Fatalism had to be counteracted with something stronger or the lack of responsibility cycle would simply continue. Sheryl and I became unalterably convinced that these kids could be lifted out of a mind-set of fatalism so we set about doing this. We reasoned that if we could empower them to believe that they were making choices, then regardless of their circumstances they could begin to make better choices. These better choices would improve their lives. We believed their lives could be changed by empowering them to reason differently. Empowerment was an idea that would be new to them. It would counteract the futility of fatalism. We knew that fatalism prevented personal power. But give them the personal power, and we would eliminate fatalism.

Two words within this first cornerstone are worth looking at more deeply. They are the words *determine* and *qualities*.

Merriam-Webster's Eleventh New Collegiate Dictionary defines *determine* as, "to decide by choice of alternatives." As I choose between two or more alternatives I determine the short term or long term future of my life. We focused on the future because of our concern with our kids' eternal destination. We knew that *future* would allow us to talk about the concept of eternity.

The word *determine* empowers me. It focuses responsibility for my life on me. When I choose between alternatives I am empowered because I am making the choice. When I make a choice I decide something about me and that makes me the most powerful person in my world.

Replace *determine* with words from its definition and the cornerstone sounds like this:

- Life is full of choices, and the choices I make today will *definitely decide* the qualities of my life...
- Life is full of choices, and the choices I make today will *establish the character of (or form)* the qualities of my life...

- Life is full of choices, and the choices I make today will *ordain* the qualities of my life...

Webster's definition of *qualities* includes "peculiar and essential character, capacity and aristocracy." Synonyms of *quality* are, "property, character and attribute."

My life is unique. I have had unique experiences and I have chosen to let those experiences affect me in ways that are unique to me. Therefore my life possesses a unique and essential character not found in anyone else.

Replace *qualities* with other words from its definition and the cornerstone sounds like this:
- Life is full of choices, and the choices I make today will determine the *peculiar and essential character* of my life...
- Life is full of choices, and the choices I make today will determine the *capacity* of my life...
- Life is full of choices, and the choices I make today will determine the *aristocracy (nobility)* of my life...

This third one fosters higher questions. "Is my life based on a higher goal?" "Am I working toward a nobler purpose?"

Replace *qualities* with its synonyms and it sounds like this:
- Life is full of choices, and the choices I make today will

determine the *property (a characteristic that belongs to a thing's essential nature when used to describe a type or species)* of my life…

- Life is full of choices, and the choices I make today will determine the *character* of my life…
- Life is full of choices, and the choices I make today will determine the *attributes* of my life…

The point is simply this: This is *my* life. *My* choices make it peculiar to *me*. Therefore, my choices will determine the essential nature of my life. My life has a unique capacity and my choices will result in the properties that set my life apart from *all* others.

Many of our Community Center kids came to us with a fatalistic viewpoint. They were convinced that if their father dropped out of school or their brother was in a gang then they had no choice but to end up the same. One of the poisons of fatalism is that once I have made a choice, I am committed to that course of action and my future is set. There is a seed of truth in this. When that seed is planted and nourished it produces an attitude mired in victim mentality.

But that seed does not have to be planted or nourished. Just as I have made poor choices that have produced negative qualities in my life, I can also make different choices to achieve better qualities. I can graft the buds of truth onto my rootstock of negativism at any time, to produce better fruit.

When I make positive choices I can overcome past negative ones and experience completely new qualities in my life. This is empowerment.

The strength of the first cornerstone is that it focuses on the choices I make right now, not the choices I made yesterday. Yesterday is gone. I cannot change it. However, I can make different choices today. The qualities of my life in the future depend on what I choose to do today.

> The qualities of my life in the future depend on what I choose to do today.

I am who I am because of the choices I've made. I can choose to stay this way if I am comfortable with the status quo. If I make bad choices, I continue to create the rut I live in. Eventually I can become incapable on my own of considering different choices. Making the same choices again and again causes me to become mired deeper and deeper in the same old negative patterns.

Deep down inside we know that what we choose to do produces the results in which we live. We have either forgotten that we are able to make new and different choices, or we simply have become comfortable with the life we currently have. There are no other options.

In the Bible, the Gospel writer, Matthew, tells the story of a rich young ruler who came to ask Jesus how to have eternal life. Jesus listened to him and then asked him to make a choice that would determine the qualities of his life. Jesus told the young man that he needed to choose between a life ruled by money and a life born of discipleship. Jesus' instructions are recorded in Matthew 19:21 (NLT): "Go and sell all your possessions and give the money to the poor, and you will have treasure in heaven. Then come, follow me." We are told the young man, upon hearing these words, "…went away sad, for he had many possessions."

That young man made the choice to permit the circumstances of life, primarily his possessions, to overpower the qualities of life he really wanted. From what he asked, it would seem that he wanted what Jesus offered, but it turned out he was unwilling to make the required choices to have the eternal life that Jesus wanted to give him.

We used this Bible story to teach that qualities of life are not determined by possessions but by the choices we make as we live in relationship with God. We used this cornerstone of Life Is Full of Choices to help our kids hear the truth, to learn that in their lives they were already making choices. We wanted to empower them by helping them realize that their choices would determine the qualities of their lives.

Our kids needed to see that consequences would occur

immediately and be imposed regularly. This understanding caused me to change my behavior. I needed to be more consistent. I had believed that consistency was made up of doing what I thought was best for me and for those around me. I came to realize that I was wrong. When dealing with kids, consistency had to be defined as, "Doing what they heard me say I would do."

The difference between these two paradigms is the perspective. The first one is mine and it is framed primarily by my knowledge of my life. The second is formed by the person I am interacting with, the one who is comparing my actions to the words I speak. He or she is not confused by my feelings or any of the things that are happening in my life. All they see are my actions and they measure my actions against my words.

I have come to believe that it is *their* view of my consistency that forms the true measure of whether or not I am consistent. This is a profound truth. I remember my mother telling me, "Actions speak louder than words." She was right.

> It is *their* view of my consistency that forms the true measure of whether or not I am consistent.

We all need consistency. For a child the need is even greater than for adults. A child sees things from a child's perspective, not an adult perspective. The child wants to know I will be consistent so they can trust me and relax within that assurance.

Consistency provides the boundary in which children can relax.

I was attending a seminar for youth workers a few years ago and one speaker said, "Consistency is so hard to achieve. My advice to you is not to even worry about it anymore. Do the best you can and be happy with that."

A few months later I was at a Sunday School Seminar. One of the presenters said almost the same exact thing about being a parent. "Consistency is just too difficult. Don't feel guilty about not being consistent; just do the best you can."

The philosophy of giving up on consistency is wrong! Professional advice that encourages expending minimum effort on being consistent and being contented with mediocre results simply promotes a lazy way out of a difficult situation.

Consistency is hard work. In fact, acting with consistency

becomes the hardest part of working with children. Achieving consistency is even harder when you are working with a staff! The simple truth is this: as hard as it is, the efforts are worth the results. The rewards of consistency are worth the commitment!

We saw this in our kids' lives. Our consistency produced a measure of calmness in them, a willingness to be open with us, and the ability to trust what we said.

We were exhausted. It was dark, I had been driving all day and we were just now dropping off the last kid we had taken to a week of youth camp. It has been a great week. We had seen many kids trust God for salvation and we had even started seeing positive changes happen from the choices kids were making.

We pulled up to the front of the house to drop off the last kid and he looked at Sheryl and started to cry: "Don't make me go home."

"Julian, what's the matter"

"I don't want to go inside; I don't want to go home. Take me somewhere else, anywhere; just don't make me go in there."

We drove down the block and parked in front of the

Community Center. Sheryl asked, "Okay, Julian, what's going on?"

During that week of camp Julian had been exposed to a consistent and caring environment. We came to learn that this was the first time he had ever experienced this, a whole week where people weren't yelling at each other, where people said "please" and "thank you" and actually cared about how the other person felt.

Julian ended up going home that night, but the power of a week of consistency had changed his perception of what life could be. A week of consistency inserted into a life of chaos, had changed this young man.

For the next few years, anytime the doors of the Center were open, Julian was there. If we went somewhere, he was ready to go. If we needed a favor, he would help.

We learned many truths about being consistent. Here are some of them:
- Consistency was not optional.
- Consistency makes a positive difference.
- Consistency is what teaching is all about!
- Consistency is what being a policeman, is all about!
- Consistency is what being a youth pastor, is all about!
- Consistency was the key to everything we wanted to accomplish with our kids.

If my words are going to have any meaning to the people I am talking to, then my actions must be consistent with my words. If they are not, then my words have no credibility and I would be better off not saying anything.

Someone was always in charge at the Community Center. Leadership abhors a vacuum. Either the adults would be in control or the children would. Consistency was the key to establishing who was in charge. When I or another adult was running things our kids learned how to act within the boundaries that we established.

The desire to relate with the kids brought challenges. The popular message was that the adult in charge needed to be friends with the kids, to go out of their way to make the kids feel good about themselves and the relationship with the authority figure. The theory was that when kids were treated this way they'd want to be around us, talk with us, and share their problems with us.

Nothing could be further from the truth.

At the Community Center we discovered that the kids didn't need more friends. What they needed were mentors, adults who could make difficult and right decisions for the longer view. The kids needed mature adults who were honest, truthful, and stable. Kids needed responsible adults to provide a safe place where children could relate to other children while growing to respect authority. All of these characteristics grow out of consistency.

Consistency was the only tool I had (yes, the only tool) that made disciplining children at the Community Center easier and effective. In groups made up of children and adults, if the adults weren't willing to regularly enforce the boundaries, children would push hard to find out what they could get away with. Allowed to continue the kids would eventually take control and the result would be chaos.

I've seen this truth in the lives of hundreds of inner city youth. I've watched kids shrivel up and withdraw into a gang because of the lack of leadership within their family. I've seen children rebel because a parent or guardian didn't exercise consistency and the kid rightly concluded the adult could not be trusted.

I've heard the same story of the same condition countless times from parents and grandparents as we have traveled around the United States. I've heard the remorse in these questions and comments: "What did I do wrong?" "I gave them everything they wanted." "I tried my best to love them."

When children are in control the choices they make are from a "me first" mentality, without much thought for the future. The parent or adult in charge has to do it differently.

The one in charge has to choose consistency. That choice affects the futures of kids and adults.

If I am working at being consistent and mess up a few times, or even make mistakes a lot of times, I can apologize and start over. But if I am not even trying then there is no standard, nothing to apologize for, and no place from which to start over.

In working with children, the most important gift I give them is my consistency.

- It is more important than my time.
- It is more important than my attention.
- It is more important than my money.
- With consistency I form foundations to build positive futures.
- Without consistency, no matter how much energy I expend, I am less effective than I should be.
- Without consistency I am not helping the children in my charge.
- Without my consistency not much changes for the good; the kids just get older without maturing.

The bottom line: Consistency *is* the key to working with kids.

3

Mending Fences

Once we realized how the kids saw us and our program Sheryl and I agreed that we had some fences to mend. We gathered everyone from the neighborhood together for a meeting. The kids were present along with their parents, some aunts and uncles, and a grandmother or two. Even a few pets showed up. In that meeting we apologized for the ways in which we had consistently *not* been meeting their expectations of us.

This meeting was humbling, and it was not fun. This was not a meeting where we just said "I'm sorry" and moved on. This meeting was a long session of relating and discussing the mistakes we had made and describing where we wanted to go from here.

We wanted to make sure our audience understood what we were talking about, so we engaged in an up-front conversation that looked and sounded like this:

- We faced the truth. "This is what we think we have done to let you down." We described where we had failed.
- We questioned, "Do you have anything to add to this list?" We noted what they said.
- We promised, "This is what we will do in the future." These were promises we intended to keep.
- We asked, "What else do we need to do?" and humbly received their input.

The kids didn't believe us and they shouldn't have believed us, at least not yet. The parents were amazed that we would even have this kind of discussion. We had spent a couple of years setting a model of letting them down. One afternoon of saying "I am going to change" did not alter our history with them or prove that we were serious.

We had to start over, beginning with recognizing and admitting patterns of behavior that we had established. While we needed to apologize, we also had to remember that actions would speak louder than words and that the truth of the apology and commitment to change was in our hands.

The eight most powerful words in the English language that can be expressed to another person, when said in this order and with integrity are, "I am sorry. Will you please forgive me?" We expressed those eight words, and meant them. Only at that moment could the relationships we really wanted to build with the kids, begin. We knew we would have to prove our words with our actions. We had to change our behaviors, first. We had to choose to be more consistent.

The transformation of our ministry with young people came when we stopped evaluating what we were doing from our perspective and started seeing or trying to see our actions from a child's perspective. Changing our perspective was the beginning of a whole new chapter for us and the kids at the Community Center.

From that day forward Sheryl and I began building new relationships with neighborhood kids, ones built on consistency. If we said it, we did it. If we couldn't do it, we apologized, tried to make up for our failure, and started over. We had become convinced that "actions speak louder than words."

4

Cornerstone Number Two — Responsibility

In the months that followed we saw progress in the lives of our kids. We also made another discovery. It was not a new one, but we relearned its truth and incorporated it into what we did. This truth concerned selfishness and how we dealt with it.

The kids we worked with were more concerned about themselves than other kids. Like almost every child they were selfish and self centered. They had a "me first" outlook on life. Most adults who have been around young kids have seen this tendency.

When our sons, Brian and Paul, were young we would put them on the floor with a plethora of toys to play with. At some point either Brian, or Paul, would be playing with a car and put it down to play with a stuffed animal, and his brother would pick up that recently discarded car. Just as soon as the car was in the brother's hand the one without the car would shout, "Mine!"

It didn't matter that there were a dozen other cars on the floor. It was of no concern that the car had become less interesting that a stuffed animal. It was still, "Mine!"

This selfish reaction is normal for a two year old. The problem comes that as kids get older some have not been taught that being the "center of the universe" is not the normal condition of life. What is normal, even expected for a two year old becomes obnoxious in a twelve year old and quite scary in a fourteen year old who can make the choice to go home and get a gun.

These kinds of stories make it onto the television nightly news far too often: the report of an intentional drive-by shooting, or the story of someone who wasn't in a gang getting shot for no reason at all. We witnessed how the kids at the Community Center were tempted to use force to express their displeasure if they got their feelings hurt. It is alarming when an adolescent still believes they are the center of the universe and resorts to violence to prove it.

We encouraged our kids to go to church on Sunday, but the churches in our community didn't want our kids. Their reasons were varied. For one, churches are supported by adults. Kids don't have much to put in the offering plate. Kids also make noise during the service, leave handprints on the walls, don't know when to stand up, when to bow their heads, when to sit down, and sometimes don't know enough not to ask for seconds when receiving Communion.

In spite of all the stuff the kids didn't grasp and couldn't contribute to, we knew that if a church chose to adopt a few of our kids into their fellowship it would change the church for the better. So we tried building relationships with local churches. We invited them to come to our events so they could meet our kids. We figured once they met them they would fall in love with the cutest kids in the whole world, and then our problem of churches refusing them would be solved.

It didn't work that way. Church people either didn't come, or they came, saw what we were doing and left never to return again, saying, "You're doing a great program!" The church people made the choice for reasons only they knew, that they didn't want our kids in their services and there was nothing we could do about it. Life is full of choices, and apparently they couldn't see that under the banner of church they were making poor choices that could produce adverse consequences in these kids' lives both now and in the future.

Involvement with the kids might have helped the church to grow beyond itself.

Since church was not a viable option Sheryl and I needed a tool we could use to spotlight a mind-set of selfishness. We wanted our kids to recognize the tendency toward selfishness and exercise making a different choice.

As a result we developed another cornerstone. In creating two cornerstones we needed a way to distinguish between them. We started calling them Cornerstone Number One and Cornerstone Number Two. While the terms weren't very original they fit the need at the time.

Cornerstone Number One had said:

> *Life is full of choices,*
> *and the choices I make today*
> *will determine the qualities of my life*
> *both now and in the future.*

Cornerstone Number Two read like this:

> *Life is full of choices,*
> *and the choices I make today*
> *can affect the circumstances of my life*
> *and other people's lives*
> *both now and in the future.*

We chose a similar format for both so that each would be easy to remember. We wanted a verse type of feeling, like a poem or a song, and when we said them we used a singsong type of delivery.

As with Cornerstone Number One we chose the words of Cornerstone Number Two very carefully. We wanted the kids to realize that not only did their choices give them power over the qualities in their own lives; we wanted them to know that other's lives were impacted by their choices.

Cornerstone Number Two showed that my choices can but not necessarily will affect the circumstances in other peoples' lives. Two key words are *affect* and *circumstances*.

Webster defines *affect* as "having an influence on." Being affected is not anywhere near having something be determined for me. *Determined* was the word we used in Cornerstone Number One to illustrate how the consequences of our choices establish our future.

Cornerstone Number Two had a different purpose.

Replace *affect* with some of its synonyms and Cornerstone Number Two sounded like this:
- Life is full of choices, and the choices I make today can *influence* the circumstances of my life and other people's lives…

- Life is full of choices, and the choices I make today can *modify* the circumstances of my life and other people's lives…
- Life is full of choices, and the choices I make today can *sway* the circumstances of my life and other people's lives…

Merriam-Webster defines *circumstance* as, "an accessory condition." In Cornerstone Number Two we no longer emphasized the qualities in a person's life. Instead we focused on the circumstances that are a part of a person's life.

Our consumer based culture has endeavored to dilute the value of the individual. It has concentrated on reducing the importance of the enduring qualities of life with the supposed value of the products one thinks they deserve. At best these tangible items are only add-ons. Two examples:

- Media advertising talks about how we deserve the objects designed to bring happiness: that special toy, those designer clothes, that fancy accessory, that brand new car.
- Television programming deals with emotions. It concerns the stuff that a person thinks will bring emotional happiness.

But these are merely circumstantial and temporary. They represent only accessories. They do not compose life itself.

If I replace *circumstances* with its synonyms, Cornerstone Number Two sounds like this:

- Life is full of choices, and the choices I make today can affect the *details* of my life and other people's lives...
- Life is full of choices, and the choices I make today can affect the *factors* of my life and other people's lives...
- Life is full of choices, and the choices I make today can affect the *conditions* of my life and other people's lives...

We are impressed with the quality of a restaurant if the food is hot and the service is good. Both of those conditions are circumstantial to our visit to the restaurant. The next time we go there their staff could be busier than when we were there before. We could have a different server. In those new situations the food might not be as hot and our service not as prompt. These factors are circumstances of our visit, not necessarily characteristics of the restaurant.

Consider Kentucky Fried Chicken (KFC). If you buy KFC's product in Florida it will be identical to the product you buy in Washington. It tastes the same because it is made in the same way. The chicken is flavored with the same eleven herbs and spices. The cleanliness of the restaurant doesn't change the chicken. The weather doesn't change the product, either. It could be snowing with a wind chill factor of 20 degrees, or 105 degrees in the shade. No matter, the chicken is the same. It doesn't matter if you eat it while it's fresh out of the fryer or later when it's cold. The essential nature, the true character of the product is the same because it is flavored and made in the same ways.

A circumstance is anything that was given to me or can be taken from me by force or another person's choice. If I just have to have that new car I get it because I think it will make me happy. Will that car continue to provide me that same level of happiness year after year? Or in a few years will there be another car that I just have to have?

If it fades, it's a circumstance.

I might be happier if I had another job. Let's say I obtain it. In a few years will this new job continue to make me happy? Or is there a chance that my new boss will drive me crazy like my old one did?

Circumstances do not determine happiness. If someone can change my circumstances then it must be concluded that I am *allowing* that person to have control over what makes me happy. If this is true, then I must question: Do I really want another person to have that kind of control over my life?

Circumstances do not determine happiness.

Characteristics of circumstances are often confused with characteristics of qualities. Here are a few areas where some think they are dealing with qualities but really they are dealing with circumstances: income, job, vehicle, family, house, school, educational degree, favorite team, awards, promotions, church, spouse, and even my life. All of these are accessory conditions.

If it fades, it's a circumstance.

The real question for my life is this: Do I want to focus on the *qualities* of my life and be in control, or do I want to focus on the *circumstances* of my life and give the power of my life to someone else?"

Here are the differences:

- Qualities are central characteristics of my life. A circumstance is an accessory condition.
- The qualities of life are permanent as long as I maintain them. A circumstance is temporary and can be taken away from me.
- The qualities found in my life determine who I am. A circumstance is what happens to me.

Cornerstone Number Two speaks to the ripple affect my

choices have on other people's circumstances and, therefore, how other people's choices can affect mine.

I control the qualities of my life. This means that other people can affect me only if I choose to allow them to do it. Therefore, it is my choice to change my life. Changing my life is not dependent upon other people's actions. So at best other people can only affect my circumstances, not the core reality of who I am or what I am worth as a person.

The application of this truth is this: How other people relate to me also applies to how I relate to them. I do not have the ability to control the qualities of another person's life, so I will not give another person the ability to control mine.

My life equals the sum of my choices. My choices add up to and become my life.

My choices add up to and become my life.

We gave Cornerstone Number Two to our kids because we wanted them to realize that the actions or words of other people did not mean that they had to respond like everyone else did when faced with a similar situation. In school, a kid may get into a fight because he was called a name. If I am called that same name, I do not have to respond with anger and fighting. I can choose to walk away.

So often the kids in the Community Center didn't see their reactions as something they had the ability to control. In fact, this was a new truth to them.

One day Caesar, age fourteen, was sitting on the front steps of the Community Center with Maria, a young lady of thirteen he was madly in love with. He had known her for at least a week. He was sure he would spend the rest of his life with her. Together they were picking out colors for their living room and choosing names for the four sons they were going to raise.

At that time Willy happened to walk by. Willy was a mature fifteen year old and had been Maria's boyfriend the week before. Seeing his former girlfriend with another kid Willy made some deriding comments that were not appreciated by Caesar. This confrontation was one Caesar had seen many times in the neighborhood. Immediately he felt he had to "defend the honor of his girl."

Caesar went home and came back with a gun.
- The fact that he was only fourteen did not matter.
- The fact that he had never shot a gun before didn't matter.

- The fact that there were twenty people on the street didn't matter.
- The fact that after fourteen shots he had only managed to graze Willy's ankle didn't matter.
- The fact that he was lucky enough not to hit anyone else, and that his poor marksmanship kept him from being tried as an adult didn't matter, either.
- What mattered to Caesar was that he had successfully "defended the honor of his future wife."

The story would have a happy ending except in the years that followed Caesar did learn how to shoot a gun with more accuracy, and he found reason to practice on other people. Caesar is now serving three life terms in prison because he never accepted the truth that he had the power to choose how he reacted. He never chose to learn that he did not have to react the same way other people did.

5

Rules and Results

Sheryl and I loved working with our kids. They were unpredictable, exciting, unmanageable, and much of the time out of control.

Of course, we had times when the kids were well behaved. They would come in, sit around some tables, play games, and we would relish the hours of relative peace and quiet. We could have long conversations about school, homework, life in the neighborhood, and family. Those were great conversations. Those times taught us much.

Other times the kids would walk through the door and havoc would reign. The windows would appear to bulge from the sudden release of pent up noise and frenetic activity after their day of school was done. Those days also taught us much — but they were not as enjoyable.

We would spend a lot of time each afternoon getting ready. We couldn't predict if the quiet kids would show up and provide a peaceful setting, or if we would soon have a room full of terror caused by the presence of unruly kids. We had to be prepared for whoever walked through our doors.

After a while of dealing with this uncertainty Sheryl and I decided we needed some way to take more control of the time these kids spent at the Community Center. It was for our sanity as well as theirs. We developed a system that would reward them for positive behavior and penalize them for negative behavior.

We came up with the Four Rules. We printed them and put them on the walls. These rules were simple enough:

- Respect God.
- Respect Yourself.
- Respect Others.
- Respect the Stuff.

We gave them $3.00 in Los Angeles Community Center Play Money for attending on any given day. They got more money for positive behavior. If they displayed negative behavior we took a dollar away from them. We rewarded the behavior we wanted to encourage.

All day, every day, the kids interacted with the rules. If they ran out of money they went home. If they had a surplus of money at the end of the day they deposited it in the Community Center Bank. Then at the end of the week they could use that play money to buy things in our store.

The rules were general enough to cover a whole host of behaviors. They were also specific enough to help the kids consider their individual actions.

Look closely at the categories. You will see that fighting, gang signs, graffiti, swearing, and throwing toys or game pieces were covered by those general categories.

Each choice of behavior carried its own consequence. Choices and consequences were posted on the wall. We wanted the kids to know them well. For example the consequence of fighting was that you were sent home. Fighting was a big No-No. The Center was designed to be a safe place for everyone. Fighting showed you were not respecting others and that you were choosing to make the place unsafe. If you made the place unsafe you had chosen to leave. You could come back tomorrow, but today you had to go home.

Swearing was classified as "not respecting God." Depending on the actual swearing that was done they might also not be respecting themselves or others. Either way the consequence of swearing was the loss of $1.00.

Different behaviors came with different consequences, but all had the same result. If you chose to behave well, you were rewarded. If you chose to misbehave, you lost money right out of your pocket.

This strategy worked. As long as the kids wanted what was available in the store they worked toward accumulating enough money to allow them to buy the stuff they wanted. Our challenge was keeping the store stocked with things they wanted! We had all kinds of candy, gum, and sweets. Over time we added school supplies, notebooks, and backpacks. Then we saw the need to add personal items like toothbrushes, toothpaste, deodorant, and shampoo. Around Christmas we obtained little things they could buy for their parents and siblings. Eventually other people heard about our store and we were given trips to Disneyland, Magic Mountain, movie tickets, and even a bicycle.

As long as each staff member was consistent, giving the same reward for the same behavior and penalizing infractions in the same way, things went well. When a new volunteer became part of our program and they were not in sync with what we were doing, it all fell apart. The most important element in making this system work was that each of us rewarded the same behaviors and penalized the same infractions.

Consistency was needed so that we all handled the play money the same way. I couldn't reward one action one day and disregard it the next. I needed to be consistent with what Sheryl was doing, too. If I rewarded a certain positive behavior by giving out dollars and she rewarded an opposite behavior in the same way, the system didn't work. It didn't matter which of us was "right." We just needed to be together in what we were doing.

As we disciplined kids in the Community Center we learned another vital truth. We never worried about their emotions or feelings. We only dealt with behaviors. It was what they did that earned rewards or got them in trouble, not how they felt and the emotions they expressed. They could pout, sulk, even sit in the corner and look angry. It didn't matter. They could feel angry as long as they didn't hit someone. Hitting was the behavior that got them into trouble. They could pout all day long as long as they did not swear at someone. Swearing was the action that got them into trouble.

We required better behavior in Bible Club. If you wanted to attend the Center on the day Bible Club was conducted you had to participate. We did our best to make it fun, active, and profitable for the kids who came. We handed out a lot of dollars there. Sheryl and I decided we didn't want any kids sitting around on the edges just watching, or worse making fun of the kids who were engaged in Bible Club, so we set the rule that if you we there you had to participate during Bible Club, even if you didn't like it.

We must have done something right. The day we conducted Bible Club was the day of the week we consistently had the most kids at the Center. All those kids presented even more opportunities to teach the truth about choices and consequences. We often referenced the Four Rules that were in plain sight.

It worked like this. When a bunch of kids would come together invariably two of them would start fighting at some point. When this would occur I would approach the kids who were fighting, separate them, and then ask one, "What choice are you making?"

I would receive a startled look because adults who are going to administer punishment usually ask, "Why?" They don't usually ask, "What choice you are making?" The kid would become confused and respond with, "What?"

I would say it again. "What choice are you making?" I could see it in his eyes. He may have been confused by my question but it was a question, and he knew how to answer a question when he knew he was getting in trouble. So, he would enter his comfort zone. The comments usually sounded like this: "I had to hit him because he called my sister…"

I would interrupt: "I understand that, but what choice are you making?"

He would start over, "You don't understand, he called my sister a name so I had to hit ..."

Again I would interrupt: "I do understand that, but what choice are you making?"

Again I would hear something like, "I didn't start this. He started it yesterday when he..."

"I understand. What choice are you making?"

"He did..."

"I understand. What choice are you making?"

"But he really did..."

"I understand. What choice are you making?"

After a number of minutes of this kind of interchange one of the boys would get it and respond, "I am choosing to go home." I would then say, "Yes, this was your choice. Have a good day. I will see you tomorrow."

I didn't have to yell. I didn't have to question what had

happened. Frankly, I didn't care what had happened or why. All I needed was for them to realize that they were making choices and that consequences would follow.

Once they recognized their choices I pointed out the consequences posted on the wall. It was no longer me kicking them out. Since they had chosen bad behavior, they had chosen to leave. I didn't have to get frustrated with them for breaking my rules. My job was to remind them that they'd chosen their behaviors and would bear the consequences of the choices they made.

We held unreservedly to the rules posted on the wall. Those rules and their consequences helped us make the Community Center a safe place for the kids who came. Because we avoided getting into power struggles with the kids, the Center became a sane place for the staff, too.

6

Introducing the Four Core Needs

Over time our kids started to make better choices. We saw it. We were there. We were often included when they expressed their feelings of elation as the "light" went on in their lives. That light was the beginning of a deeper understanding. It was wonderful!

That "light" was usually evident the moment a child would say:

- "What will you do if I choose to...?"
- "You mean it is my choice to say or do something and you will still like me?"
- "I don't want to choose whether to do this or that. That is too much responsibility. Just tell me what to do."

When we heard the word *choice* in a child's vocabulary we knew that child was starting to see life as they would a movie, but instead of just watching the movie that young person was acting as the movie's director!

The two cornerstones had become foundational truths. Placing these principles into a child's life allowed that child to start to build their life upon them. We knew that without these cornerstones our kids would be influenced and affected by circumstances and their emotional needs of the moment.

A cornerstone is a part of the foundation of a structure, of course. A foundation determines the size, shape, and the integrity of the building it supports.

We believed that if you gave a kid a solid foundation that child could build a stronger life. If the foundation was cracked or crooked the life built upon it could not stand tall or straight. Each of the cornerstones became part of the firm foundation upon which a child could construct his life. Cornerstone Number One built a structure of empowerment. Cornerstone Number Two built a structure of responsibility.

This concept and application were working well, but the more Sheryl and I applied these truths with the Community Center kids the more we realized we didn't have all the knowledge we needed. To reach into their lives and affect lasting change we had to understand them at a deeper level.

We needed some insight into what made them tick.

One day I was playing a card game with a group of kids at the Center. The object of the game was to match colors or numbers on the cards. The kids loved playing this game because it was fast and everyone had an equal chance of winning.

I decided to observe the actions of the kids around me from a new perspective. I wanted to see what their actions would reveal about their emotional needs. My goal was to unravel codes of behavior to better equip me to interact with them in a caring way. For example, I knew that if a child wanted more love and affection they would stay closer to me and be tender.

I chose the term *core needs* to identify what I saw. I knew the term was not new. It was certainly not a new concept, either. I realized the phrase was employed to describe characteristics of diverse applications such as nutrition, housing, government services, education, and even income.

I used the term with a renewed focus, however. I wanted to understand a child's emotional core needs by observing that child's actions and reactions. I was endeavoring to identify their desires for satisfaction that motivated their behavior.

I came back to the adage that actions speak louder than

words. These kids might not tell me what they needed emotionally, but I reasoned that if I could figure out what they received when they acted a certain way, then I could go right to the need instead of dealing with peripheral issues.

In the quest to bridge emotional need with observable behavior I collected comparable ideas from other people. Here are a couple of them. I added the italics.

- In her book entitled *Instinctive Parenting* released in March of 2010, author Ada Calhoun stated that she had "...found some sanity by staying focused on her son's *core needs* of shelter, food and love."
- Kathy Koch founded an organization called Celebrate Kids, Inc. in July of 1991. Their purpose statement starts by saying, "Celebrate Kids, Inc. is dedicated to helping parents, educators, and children of all ages meet their *core needs* of security, identity, belonging, purpose, and competence."

Authors and leaders look differently at the needs of the kids with whom they work. They come up with distinct descriptions as well as unique ways to classify and deal with them. We did the same. In our application the cornerstones made up the foundations our kids could use to build their lives upon lasting principles. Understanding and meeting their emotional core needs allowed our kids to construct their own lives upon those cornerstones. The cornerstones were the building blocks. The core needs represented the effects life had on our kids. We chose to do what we could to meet their core needs which in turn gave them a chance to appropriate the lessons from the cornerstones.

We identified and labeled the Four Core Needs:
1. Affection
2. Boundaries
3. Consistency
4. Discipline

When children's four core needs are satisfied the kids are better able to start working on constructing their lives. When those core needs are unmet the kids spend their time and energy finding ways to meet those needs through the people with whom they come in contact on a daily basis.

The Four Core Needs color a child's entire existence. Understanding these needs empowers those who work with the kids to make sense of their behaviors and deal with them more effectively.

The Four Core Needs strongly influence how a child perceives their surroundings and what happens within them. Everything we did *for* our kids, *with* our kids, and *to* our kids, was interpreted *by* our kids on the basis of the Four Core Needs.

Because these needs colored their paradigm the kids

saw my actions from a wholly different perspective, theirs. Their perspective often did not match how I wanted to be seen. Differing perspectives influenced and framed their interpretations.

I came to realize that if I wanted to work with these kids I had to acquire an informed understanding of their views and what they meant. I had to learn why it was that when I did one thing they often thought I was trying to accomplish something else.

For instance, in working with any group of kids at the Community Center it was a fairly common occurrence to see one of the group do something that would result in that child being sent home. Fighting, stealing, swearing, throwing something in the building, or not picking up your mess, could result in the perpetrator being sent home.

Shortly after a kid had been sent home it was also fairly common for a parent or grandparent to show up at our front door. "Why are you picking on my son?" was usually the way the conversation started. After explaining the activity the child had been involved in, showing them the rules and the consequences for breaking those rules posted on the wall, the conversation usually ended with, "Well, I'd better have a talk with little Jimmy." A perspective could only be understood when accurate information was given and received.

I vividly remember the day I discovered someone had dumped a car in our parking lot. It happened over a weekend. It was not unusual for people to spend time working on their cars on neighborhood streets. It was also not unusual for people to park their cars under the trees that lined the side of our building because working in the shade was just more comfortable. That weekend a shade tree mechanic had cut the chain to our gate and had moved his "shop" into our parking lot.

When I arrived on Monday morning, the car, or what remained of it, was the first thing I noticed. You couldn't miss it. Most of the engine was gone, the windows were broken out, and the interior was trashed. That shade tree mechanic or some neighborhood kids had removed the tires, wheels, and the hubs of their rusted, broken down hulk of a car. The result was that we couldn't easily tow it away. The remnant rested on its frame in the middle of our parking lot.

After finding out how much it would cost to pay someone to tow it away on a flat bed truck I spent the next week talking to one government agency after another. I was ping-ponged back and forth, hearing one bureaucrat say, "That is quite a problem. It's not my department's responsibility. Why don't you talk to...?" Each bureaucrat directed me to another one. Eventually I was directed back to the first person who had pointed me to someone else!

I spent a week tossing queries around City Hall. Finally one of the faceless government employees said to me, "It is too bad it is sitting on your parking lot. If it was on the street, the city could pick it up within a couple hours." Soon I was jacking up this hulk of a car. I put a series of pipes under it and rolled it on the pipes out onto the street. As I got the car onto the street a guy came by and yelled at me about leaving my trash in the street, saying that was why the neighborhood was falling apart, asking how could I do that to the people who live and work in this community? Huh?

Here I was trying to *improve* the neighborhood, clean up the streets, and have a positive influence on the kids who lived there, and I was the one getting yelled at by some guy who was completely ignorant about my efforts to clean up someone else's junk. He didn't believe it wasn't my car, that it was my neighborhood, and that I was just trying to do the best I could. But at least the city came when I called and removed the trash.

The point is this: my actions were not interpreted through my lens of reality. My actions were perceived and interpreted through someone else's reality. A parent hears that their son is being disciplined for something. That parent believes their kid couldn't have done this in the first place and then accuses me of being unfair to their perfect little Jimmy. The guy who is not familiar with East Los Angeles concludes that a white guy towing a junker means that I am the problem instead of trying to be part of the solution.

This is all about our point of view—our paradigm—and how that paradigm colors the world around us. We see things from this paradigm naturally because it's the frame of reference we know and understand. We evaluate our needs and those of others from this perspective because it is the one closest to us.

Kids know their world and see their needs within their world. I use the term *core needs bank account* to describe this. This idea of a bank account illustrates how every interaction with another person produces a positive or negative effect on their core needs account. If their core needs are met it's a deposit into their account, if the core needs are not met, it's a withdrawal.

This idea helps me see that kids place a value on every interaction we have with them. It was certainly true at the Community Center. Every time they felt we'd had a positive interaction with them a deposit had been made into their core needs bank account. Every time they felt we'd had a negative interaction a withdrawal had been made from that account.

As we worked to become more consistent we discovered it wasn't just one bank account into which we were making deposits into a kid's life. What we came to envision was broader in scope. Instead of a single bank account we saw the areas of core needs within each of our kid's lives represented by four separate accounts. Each of the Four Core Needs had its own bank account in each child. We were having a positive or negative effect on each account for every kid, all the time.

The innate desire for every kid is to have a healthy balance in all four accounts. This bank account metaphor may not have been readily understood by the kids, but it was clear to us. It helped us understand the importance and effects of core needs deposits and withdrawals in the lives of the kids. When something positive would happen in a child's life the amount in one bank account would increase. When the child perceived something negative was happening the amount in the account would go down.

The children with whom we worked instinctively knew whether or not their core needs were being met. At any given moment they were making choices about how to conduct their lives in efforts to increase the amount in their emotional account that had the lowest balance at the time.

A child who experiences a withdrawal from one of their emotional core needs accounts feels that a piece of their life has gone missing. A close friend or family member might not even notice this disparity. Perhaps that friend or family member has simply become used to relating to that kid in an emotional vacancy. But this void can be very obvious to someone else observing from the outside. The person who cares could very well see that an emotional vacuum was present and that it needed to be filled.

We will deal with the Four Core Needs of Affection, Boundaries, Consistency, and Discipline one at a time. We will endeavor to see why each Core Need is vital to a child's emotional development in building a balanced life. We will learn how the Four Core Needs cooperate with the Three Cornerstones and contribute to a child's wellbeing.

7

Affection

We define *affection* as, "anything we do to make a child feel good about him or herself." One recognized emotional need within our culture today is the need for a loving touch. But a little history might be in order to see how that idea has not always been universally accepted.

Quoted from *The Vital Touch: How Intimate Contact With Your Baby Leads To Happier, Healthier Development* by Sharon Heller, Ph.D.: "Spoiling: The concept of spoiling an infant by holding them or responding quickly to their cries was 'invented' by the behaviorist John Watson. His views were published in 1928 in his book, *The Psychological Care of Infant and Child*. His advice was very severe, 'Never hug and kiss them [children], never let them sit in your lap. If you must, kiss them once on the forehead when they say good night.'

"For more than 20 years, *Infant Care*, published by the U.S. Children's Bureau, warned mothers to avoid at all cost picking up baby between feedings, lest they create a 'spoiled, fussy baby.' In this country, as late as the beginning of the twentieth century, orphans received little caressing. Almost 100 percent of them died. Now called nonorganic failure-to-thrive, infants deprived of nurturant touch often fail to grow even if hospitalized and fed enough calories intravenously.

"Dr. J. Brenneman, a hospital pediatrician, introduced a rule in his hospital that every baby should be 'picked up, carried around, and "mothered" several times a day.' Thanks to 'mothering' by 1938 mortality rates for infants at Bellevue Hospital in New York City fell within one year from around 35 percent to less than 10 percent."

Dr. Jenn Berman, author of *SuperBaby: 12 Ways to Give Your Child a Head Start in the First 3 Years*, in her article *How Touch Improves Your Baby's Development* stated, "A positive touch communicates love, acceptance, worthiness, and safety to an infant. Without it, a child is likely to die."

Thankfully John Watson's ideas on how to raise our kids were only in print for about twenty years and thankfully, most people are drawn to babies. Usually infants are held and touched with plenty of love and affection, early and often.

But touch is only one aspect of love. When I first started working on naming the four needs I soon realized that many connotations accompany the term *love*. Often these can be misunderstood, even abused. The word *love* is used in lots of ways. We fall in and out of love, real fast. I love my mother. I love French fries. I love the way this shirt makes me look. I love the current singer on *American Idol*—at least until next year when I love the next one even more.

Additional terms further confuse the meaning of this word. Love and sex are sometimes used as synonyms. Love and commitment are used interchangeably, too. Is love a state of being, a sacrificial act, or a fleeting thrill? Well, yes.

Love has many versions and perversions. I needed another term for the first core need. I tried using the word *attention* but that word just didn't seem to fit, either. I struggled with the reality that kids need and respond to attention, but not all attention is positive. There is negative attention. Some kids are so starved for attention that they will act badly in order to get noticed and yelled at. Clearly that attention is negative and not desirable. Use of the word in "getting somebody's attention" or "giving someone the attention they deserve" didn't express the true nature of the core need I was trying to describe.

Finally I chose to call the first core need *affection*. When we give our child a hug he feels good. When we buy him new jeans to wear to school, he feels cared for, he feels good about himself. When we fix dinner his stomach is full. That satisfaction translates into affection and it doesn't matter if the menu was a steak or a peanut butter and jelly sandwich.

Affection, by definition, is positive. It is a core need no matter the age. Infants need affection. So do four year olds even though the four year old may not be as cute as the newborn baby. At four years old the child has a mind of his own and a voice to express it, too. Regardless, that child still has a need for affection.

The need for affection grows as the child does. Think about the seven year old, the latchkey child. In many instances this kid is left alone for a few hours every day after school. How is he filling the void in his life that can only be satisfied by affection? Later, at age ten or eleven a gang may recruit him. The gang provides an identity in a group of his peers. The gang also provides camaraderie and a feeling of safety in a world that is normally unsafe. The gang is a poor substitute for affection but in some ways it fills the needs for identity, friendship, and safety. As a preteen that child had the same need for affection as when he was an infant, at age four or age seven. Now at ten years of age the kid thinks joining a gang is a good idea probably because he is not getting his daily quota of affection at home.

Our culture fears the perversion of adults "loving children" inappropriately so laws decree that schools can't provide any positive affection for the kids. Churches are reticent to show affection, too, or don't know how to give it in a healthy way. Since so many kids nowadays don't have extended family in close proximity many of these kids do not get the consistent, healthy affection they want and require.

The need for affection in each stage of life is expressed differently but it still is the same need. Have you ever wondered how a young teenager could make the mistake of getting pregnant or fathering a child? Mostly, these serious errors are cries for affection. Desires to meet that need become stronger than the understanding of what the future might hold when a young person becomes a single parent and a child is born into an uncertain future.

Frankly the kids who choose this path don't care about their future. They are concrete thinkers. They want to make a deposit in their affection account now! Have you ever met a young teenager who has chosen to be identified with a gang? Whether they actually joined the group or were just dressing or talking like a gangster didn't really matter. From their perspective the effect would be the same. You could wonder, "Why would they join a gang?" or "Why would they act like that?" The reason is they are looking for affection. Kids join a gang or dress like gangsters because they want attention from the people with whom they come in contact every day.

Attention from other kids gives them the recognition they want. However, attention is a poor substitute for the real need, the need for affection.

> Attention is a poor substitute for the real need, the need for affection.

I was developing a relationship with Jaime. Jaime was eleven years old. He was regularly coming to the after school program and was a great kid—lots of fun and he had a great sense of humor. One day he wasn't there. We didn't see him all week or the next week. Then one day he returned. It was good to see him back. We asked, "How are you?" "How are school, your mom, and sister?" "We haven't seen you for a while." "What has been going on?"

He said, "I've been going to the recreation center down the street for the past few weeks." We talked about that place. It sounded fantastic! If I were a kid, that's where I would want to go. That organization had been adopted by the Los Angeles Dodgers. The facility had a *row* of pool tables, a *row* of ping-pong tables, and a *row* of foosball tables. Jaime said they had so much stuff that there was almost never a time you had to wait to use one of the tables. Their stock of stuff made our one pool table, one ping-pong table, and one foosball table look anemic. Our kids had to sign up in order to take turns playing on one of the tables — that was the only way we could maintain order.

In all this talking, Jaime finally got to his nugget of truth. He said, "Yeah, that's a great place to be, but here, you are interested in me. You treat me like someone special. There, I am just a number." Jaime had the choice to go to an after school program where he had access to all the toys and gadgets a kid could want. Instead he came back and chose to spend his afternoons at a place that was understaffed, under funded, and under supplied because here he had found affection.

I fondly recall the story of Norma. She was a grandmotherly lady who wanted to visit the Community Center and see what we were doing. She demonstrated a loving spirit and she felt she would just love the kids. We believed she could give the kids lots of affection. So we set up a Friday night when she could come over. We met her in the parking lot. We took her upstairs and found a comfortable chair where she could interact with the kids. She looked very comfortable, at least until we opened the doors and the kids came in.

In an instant the look in her eyes changed from "loving and kind" to "scared to death." There were close to twenty teenagers occupying about 1,000 square feet of space, but to look at Norma you would think we were inside a 4' x 4' closet.

Over the next ten minutes she gradually slid her chair backwards to get farther away from the center of noise and activity, and eventually ended up in a corner. To her credit she never turned and faced the corner. Instead she kept her attention on what was happening in the room. She may have been afraid but deep down inside I believe she wanted to be a part of what was going on. Whatever her reasoning, she sat in that corner, eventually pulled some knitting out of a bag, and was content to be inconspicuous.

Her presence might have been inconsequential had not Daryl noticed that something was going on in the corner. Daryl was a huge kid for only fifteen years of age and his size intimidated everyone who knew him. Daryl lumbered over to Norma and just stood there for a couple of minutes, looking down on her, watching her knit. The longer he watched the more she intensely focused on her craft and the closer the needles got to her nose.

Eventually Daryl said, "What 'cha doing?" Norma broke her concentration and looked up through her eyelashes just long enough to say, "Knitting" before her concentration was back on her needles as they edged even closer to her nose. Everything about her tone and body language screamed, "Go away!" Daryl, however, pulled up a chair and quietly asked, "Can you teach me?"

The needles stopped. Norma sat back and looked at Daryl for a short minute then asked, "What did you say?"

"I asked, 'Can you show me how to do that?'"

Like any good grandmother Norma reached into her bag and pulled out some yarn and another set of needles. Within a couple of minutes Daryl was sitting alongside her receiving a lesson in the fine art of knitting. Within another five minutes four other teenage boys joined the group and were trying to master the language and actions of "casting on," "purl," and "slip stitch."

I didn't join the group. I was busy watching the magic of teenage boys discovering a moment of affection in a most surprising way. It wasn't about learning how to knit. I doubt any of them still know how to knit and they probably don't even remember trying to learn the art. That evening wasn't about knitting, of course; it was about affection. I believe their lives were enriched in special ways from experiencing the affection of a grandmother who overcame her own fears to share her love.

8

Boundaries

The second core need is the need for boundaries. We define *boundaries* as, "the pre-arranged limits that are placed on behavior." Boundaries come in many forms. The person establishing the boundaries has to choose where they need to be placed.

For children, boundaries can be bedtime, obedience to house rules, establishing when to be home from school or a date, how to clean up the kitchen after dinner, how to address people around you, the acceptable language to use, etc. The list of necessary boundaries in a child's life can be lengthy.

One boundary we had established at the Community

Center was that swearing was not allowed. You remember: If a kid swore it cost them one dollar out of their Community Center money. It was a great boundary, but it needed definition. We had to decide what words were classified as swear words. At one staff meeting the staff sat around for a couple hours deciding this. That was an interesting meeting.

We did well with this boundary until one day someone started swearing in Spanish. Not all the staff knew Spanish so we had a problem. We had to take the list of what the staff considered to be swear words, and translate that list into Spanish. Since they didn't teach me many swear words in Missionary Language School this involved an embarrassing time of getting the parents involved in updating our list. Then we created more staff meeting memories by conducting a class to teach all the staff how to swear in Spanish. The point: You can't set a boundary about swearing if you don't know the words they use.

Adults have boundaries, too. Freeway speed limit signs read 65. Now everyone in Los Angeles knows that 65 really means 70 because in Los Angeles police don't stop you unless you are going more than five miles an hour above the speed limit. So 65 is really just a suggestion because the real speed limit is 70. Reaching a speed of 71 can bring consequences. These consequences include red lights, being pulled over and an awkward conversation with a police officer, signing a traffic ticket, and paying a fine. The public humiliation of red lights may be bad enough but it is the fine that really gets your attention. You have to sit down and write a check (real money) and give it to someone else.

Boundaries are neither negative nor positive. They just are. The result of choosing to cross a boundary (the consequence) is often negative. But you can also experience a positive result (also a consequence) for good behavior. In either case a person who approaches a boundary chooses to respect it or violate it. That choice to honor or ignore the boundary produces negative or positive consequences.

Positive consequences are many. Here are a few:
- Your auto insurance company gives you a good driver discount for not being in an accident this year
- Your company gives you a bonus based on profit
- You get an award for not missing work
- You receive a raise for outstanding performance

Some examples of negative consequences are:
- Jail time that comes after being caught stealing
- The ticket for speeding
- Getting fired for coming to work late
- Being grounded for not cleaning your room

Setting boundaries and consequences is about building character and learning how to make healthy choices. Discipline is the process of consistently applying results for behaviors that cross a boundary. Boundaries and discipline cannot be separated.

On the introductory pages *discipline* was defined as, "the actions that are taken to instill in a child the understanding of right and wrong." We will discuss discipline more thoroughly in Chapter 10. Suffice now to say that at the Community Center discipline was all about the results that happen in a child's life that are directly related to the child's choices. The application of discipline when boundaries were broken was not about me, my position, my life, how I felt, or what was best for me. It was about respect for the boundary and the consistency of the consequence. Remember, boundaries just are.

This truth may be hard to accept and apply because society continues to send conflicting messages about how to raise and discipline our kids. The media, self help books, and our educational system tell us we need to be a "friend" to our children, we need to encourage them and build up their self-esteem at all costs. On the surface encouraging kids and building their self esteem sounds good, but no one is telling us *how* to do this and *still* maintain order in the home, the community, and the world in which we live.

Because I am the adult who is establishing and enforcing boundaries and consequences I should have already learned that I am not the center of the universe. Applying rules and consequences is not about me. I should be the mature one. I should be able to make choices about discipline that are not based on whether the child will like the boundary or the consequence of crossing it, or whether he will like me when I apply the consequence. I should be committed to doing what I think is best for the child. My purpose is to help the child grow and become a productive adult. It's all about *them*.

As an adult I am supposed to instill in my child an understanding of right and wrong. Sometimes my best efforts toward this goal are met with signals from society that are confusing. Far too often our kids witness contradictory definitions about what is right and what is wrong. It is hard to teach the knowledge of right and wrong when kids observe police breaking traffic laws, politicians excusing inappropriate or illegal behavior, or Post Office vehicles parked in no parking zones, all of which I observe or hear about almost every day.

From a child's perspective, boundaries are wanted, even needed. Kids want to know what they can get away with without getting into trouble. In fact, all of us want to know where our boundaries are.

As we developed our patterns of behavior with the kids in the Community Center I had to learn this truth: "A boundary without a consequence is a suggestion."

> A boundary without a consequence is just a suggestion.

I drive the freeways in Los Angeles and I know that a speed limit of 65 miles per hour is just a suggestion. I see lots of people passing me when I am going that speed. So I speed up to stick with traffic and soon I am going 70. I've learned that when a speed limit sign says 65 police don't write tickets if my speed exceeds the stated limit by one, two, or three miles an hour. After some trial and error I finally discovered where the true boundary is. A speed of 71 is okay but I am really careful about driving 72!

Therefore, the posted speed limit of 65 is a suggestion not a boundary. The boundary is the speed at which the police actually start writing tickets. Remember "actions speak louder than words." The posted speed limit sign shows the words. The actions that speak louder than words are the siren and red lights telling me to pull over.

Since adults test the boundaries of their world why should I expect different behaviors from the Community Center kids? When Sheryl and I gave them a reasonable boundary they would immediately test us. They wanted to see if we really understood where the boundary was and, more importantly, if we would really enforce that boundary with the agreed consequences if the boundary was violated.

The interaction looked like this: Someone would approach a boundary and look at us to see if we are paying attention. They would get as close to the edge of the boundary as they could and then, at some point while still looking at us they would move one toe just over the line. If we reacted by imposing the consequence that we had already decided upon, they would protest. Protesting was natural. Did we think they would be glad they were getting into trouble? No! But deep down they would be glad they knew we were paying attention and cared enough to enforce the boundary. Even though they didn't like negative consequences at least they knew we loved them enough to be consistent.

A pattern developed. After the kids had proven to themselves that we were paying attention they would test the boundary again just to see if we still cared enough to pay attention. Their test didn't happen immediately, maybe not even the next day. But they would repeat their actions just to make sure we were still noticing them.

Depending on your child's personality they may test you two or three times, or they may test you twenty or thirty times. Robert MacKenzie in his book, *Setting Limits with Your Strong Willed Child* uses a phrase I like. He says that some people are "hard-way learners." That phrase explains a lot. The ends of a continuum are formed by "soft-way learners" and "hard-way learners." Learning styles are present all along the line but somewhere to the left of center the hard-way learners become more obvious. These are the people who aren't willing to take "No" for an answer.

I tell my hard-way learner don't touch the electrical outlet and the first thing I know, he is putting a screw driver into the electrical opening. I tell my hard-way learner not to touch the stove and before I can turn around his hand is going for the burner. It is not that they are bad kids; it's just that this is the way they learn. They need repetition for an idea to sink in. Their goal is to push the boundary to make sure you meant what you said, to test the limits, and to know you mean business.

During this process of hard-way learning should you ever fail their test they will push the boundary even more to discover the new line of unacceptable behavior. They will inch forward, keeping one eye on you and the other eye on the territory they have just gained. It may seem like their goal is to get away with as much as they can, but their real goal is to find out the point at which you will react.

What kids are looking for is the boundary. Set it with words. Enforce it with action. Actions speak louder than words. If words are not followed with action then listening stops. Consequential actions solidify the boundary and provide security.

In that sense, setting boundaries is a two-edged sword.

One edge of the sword is the fact that boundaries must be age-sensitive. They have to be reasonable. As adults, we need to make sure that they are. Recognize the difference between reasonable and unreasonable boundaries. To illustrate an unreasonable boundary: At one point the staff discussed what we could do about the boys who chose to buy their pants overly large and wear them almost falling off their hips. These young men never wore belts and often there would be an accident when the pants would fall too low for decency. We considered that we could provide belts and make them put on a belt when they walked through the door.

There were problems with this solution, however, not the least of which was how to take the belt off of them when they were leaving the Community Center and what would happen when they were outside playing basketball or some other game. The "make them wear a belt" rule when they came into the Center did not solve the need for their pants to cover their underwear when they were playing outside.

Eventually we decided that trying to change the style of clothing they chose to wear at the Center would be unreasonable. Being consistent with a boundary about pants would become a nightmare for us. We chose to not make a rule about pants or belts or underwear. Instead, we selected some of the leaders and talked with them about decency, modesty, and the image that was being presented with the styles they chose. We suggested to these leaders that they could start a new trend if they chose to make some pointed comments just at the moment a pair of pants started showing more than they would want their sister to see. We avoided trying to establish an unreasonable boundary. Instead we chose peer pressure. That kind of influence can be wonderful when you use it to promote a positive result.

Of course, we could not use peer pressure for everything. Selecting a boundary has boundaries, as well. We learned this truth: For a boundary to be reasonable, the one we chose had to be tied to the problem and the person. Boundaries will not change behaviors that are natural parts of growing up. As a child's understanding grows, however, setting appropriate boundaries becomes a necessary responsibility of whoever is in charge.

> For a boundary to be reasonable, the one we chose had to be tied to the problem and the person.

Carefully setting boundaries is the first edge of the sword. Following through on the consequences is the other. Once the rules are set they must be adhered to, and results for obedience or disobedience must be consistent.

The one in charge must be careful with the boundaries they set and the language they use to define the terms. It is the adult's responsibility to stick to the boundaries once they are established. When a boundary is crossed, if the adult does not apply the consequence, the result in a child's life is worse than not having any boundary at all.

If you are the parent of a teenager you may have established a curfew for your child. Let's say you set the curfew for 10:00 PM. You may have set the consequence of breaking the curfew, stating that violating it would result in grounding. Things could be going well when one night your child shows up five minutes late. You could say to yourself, "That's okay; it's only five minutes."

The next time it's ten minutes, and then it becomes twenty-five. Soon your teen comes home two hours past curfew because you repeatedly made allowances like, "Well, it is only a few minutes later than last night."

In this illustration sooner or later the parent will have to decide whether to have a conversation with the child about the 10:00 PM curfew that has now morphed into "whenever you want to get home" permission, or to just let it go. The parent's reasoning could go like this: "After all, it has been so long, and he has gotten away with so much. But he's a good kid and it would be hard to now go back and say he has to be home at 10:00 PM. Re-imposing a hard curfew wouldn't be fair, would it?"

The problem here is not one of fairness. A boundary is not fair or unfair, it just *is*. The kid had heard and understood that there was a 10:00 PM curfew and then systematically tested that boundary to see what the parent would do. The teen also systematically tested the parent to find out if the adult was serious about what was originally said. Remember "actions speak louder than words." In this illustration, the teenager was looking for action not permission.

The child was looking for the boundary and it wasn't there. The parent had done the work of setting up the boundary. The parent even talked about what would happen if the curfew was violated, but the parent became distracted because there wasn't sufficient belief that the boundary was important.

Boundaries *are* important. Once set, they must be respected. If violated, consequences must be consistently applied.

9

Consistency

In working with children we define *consistency* as, "doing what you said you would do." Kids are concrete thinkers. The need for consistency is even greater for them than it is for adults. Remember, children see things from a child's perspective, not an adult's perspective. They want to know that consistency is present so they can relax within the boundaries.

I recall the day David was chewing gum as he came into the Community Center. One of the big rules we had was no gum chewing in the building. We had just installed a brand new tile floor and I didn't want to be on my hands and knees scraping gum off the floor. The rule was this: NO GUM CHEWING IN THE CENTER. David knew the rule.

Everyone knew the rule. It was posted right on the wall. We even had a garbage can located right outside the front door of the Community Center so the kids could spit out their gum before they entered.

As David walked through the door I looked up from the math project I was working on with another kid and saw him chewing gum. He looked at me and saw me looking at him. Okay, so now the stage was set. He knew the rule. I saw him breaking the rule. He saw me observing him, so everyone involved knew what was going on. At that moment I said to myself: "David is a good kid. He knows the rules. I don't need to say anything to him because he will spit his gum out." A minute later I looked up and David was gone. The next day I did not see him and I didn't see him the day after that, either.

About a week later I spotted him walking down the street as I was driving home. I stopped and said, "I haven't seen you for a few days. What is going on?" He taught me a lesson I will never forget when he said, "I didn't think it mattered to you whether I came to the Community Center. The other day when I was there and you didn't say anything to me about my gum I realized that you didn't care about me since I was not even important enough to get in trouble." I thought I was paying him a compliment by not saying anything, and he saw it as an insult.

Kids need consistency and I had blown it. My lack of consistency had caused uncertainty in David's life. That one action also caused confusion as to where the boundary was.

I apologized to David. Later someone asked if I ever explained myself to him. No. An explanation would have made me feel better, but would have done nothing for him. My purpose for being at the Community Center was for his benefit, not mine. I started with an apology, not an explanation.

After the apology I had to start rebuilding the trust I had severed. That took a long time. It is hard to earn the trust of a broken child and it is even harder to reestablish trust after it has been broken. In this case it was months before I felt we had reestablished the trust we once had.

> It is hard to earn the trust of a broken child and it is even harder to reestablish trust after it has been broken.

That may have been the first time I realized how important consistency was. I had always known it was good for me to be consistent. At that moment I started to realize that what I would accomplish in these kid's lives was dependent on how consistent I was.

I also began to understand the power of an apology. Not a public apology to a group of people, but a private apology when you say to another person with total sincerity, "I am sorry. Will you please forgive me?" Those eight simple words, when used sincerely and with humility, possess the power to penetrate all the confusion and trauma that make up a difficult situation. They go to the core of the hurt and can allow a process of healing to begin.

With David I could have responded by criticizing his perceptions of what had happened, or his feelings that came from those perceptions. Either way I would have been asserting my superiority over him instead of admitting my mistake. The only way to start rebuilding the relationship was to go back to the instant of my error and create the foundation necessary to rebuild the trust he had lost in me.

Trust is built on consistency. I can't trust someone who is not consistent. You can't, either. Broken promises produce disenchantment, distrust, and resentment no matter a person's age. Grownups need consistency as much as our children do—maybe even more.

Many times I have found myself falling into the emotional quicksand of asking "why" when addressing bad behavior. Once that question is asked of a child there is almost no way to keep consistency intact. Asking the "why" question opens all kinds of doorways into diversionary topics, and all of them detract from the central point. Asking "why?" leads the kid and me through a confusing maze of unending and unanswerable questions, and there is no escape. For example, when I ask "Why?" here are some responses:

"My mother made me do…"

"I didn't get to eat lunch because the kid next to me…"

"At recess today my teacher wouldn't let me …"

"That girl over there said…"

"The ball slipped…"

"The car wasn't there a minute ago."

It doesn't really matter what the answer to the 'why' question is, the result is the same. The answer to the 'why' question is generally someone or something else. I am sucked into feeling sorry for the kid and find myself starting to look for a way out of bestowing the required consequence. I feel like the bad guy when I have to apply it because I have to ignore "what is happening in his life." I am in between a rock and a hard place. If I administer the consequence it looks like I don't care. If I don't dole out the consequence then my consistency is undermined.

For a child, there seldom is a good answer to the question, "Why?" Kids are concrete thinkers and *why* is an abstract thinker's release valve. Most of the time the best they can do is answer, "I don't know." My intentions may be positive when I consider asking, "Why?" I reason that asking why shows empathy, that I am trying to understand, that I want to help change something for the child. It's an interesting theory, but it's not realistic. Asking why may satisfy me, but doesn't do the kid any good.

10

Discipline

Discipline is defined as, "the actions that are taken to instill in a child the understanding of right and wrong in order to shape their character so they learn how to make healthy choices."

If *affection* is so vital that an infant will die if he doesn't get it, if *boundaries* are so important that a child will push the limits and then push them again to find out where the boundary is, and if *consistency* is essential to grow a healthy self image and maintain order in a child's life, then *discipline* is the confirmation that a child's life has value in the eyes of the adults who care for them. Discipline is proof that parents or guardians love a child. When discipline is administered it shows that the child is worth the parent's time and effort.

Discipline is more effective in a balanced and trustworthy atmosphere where an affection-based relationship is present, boundaries are known and can be relied upon, and consistency is prevalent in the child's life. If discipline is absent the possibility of growing productively, is slim. Where it is done correctly it helps grow a mature individual.

Discipline rightly administered is not abuse. *Abuse* is defined as, "to use improperly or excessively" according to Merriam-Webster. Discipline used incorrectly can morph into abuse. Discipline that is uncontrolled can become abuse.

At the Community Center we believed and promoted a well thought out philosophy and practice of discipline. In this environment the responsible adult was totally in control of his or her emotions at all times. Effective discipline was not needlessly forceful, nor was it violent. It was against California state law for us to use physical contact in any way to discipline the kids, but we still had to find ways to discipline them.

Discipline could be administered as the loss of a privilege, a time out, marking a chart, or adding a job. In order for it to be effective it didn't need to be physical, it just needed to be consistent.

This kind of discipline works. It works because conse-quences for every situation that could be imagined are carefully thought out and spoken about *in advance*. This pre-dis-position helps both adult and child. When the child tests a boundary and steps over the line the consequences of doing so are already framed.

Discipline should be applied thoughtfully and pragmatically. Discipline should be composed of measured responses to negative actions of another person, in order to bring about a change in that person's behavior.

> Discipline should be composed of measured responses to negative actions of another person, in order to bring about a change in that person's behavior.

The goal of discipline is always changed and improved behavior. If the consistent application of discipline is not working toward positive behavioral change, then what is being applied is not discipline—it is either punishment or retribution!

> The goal of discipline is always changed and improved behavior.

As adults we use discipline every day. Discipline, or the threat of it, is used on us every day. When I am driving and make a sudden turn that displeases the driver of another car the offended driver honks his horn. That honk is a form of discipline. It's a degree of public humiliation. To some degree it works because I react by feeling embarrassed or defensive.

The time clock, the alarm clock, and the paycheck are additional forms of discipline. All of these items help control our actions or help other people control them.

Think about the first half of the definition we used for discipline, "The actions that are taken to instill in a child the understanding of right and wrong..." If we stop here we get children who act well only when the authority figure is in the room. They are focused on them and the discipline they can administer. They want to please, so they act as they know the adult wants them to act.

Dolores was an actively disobedient ten year old kid, the perfect example of a "hard-way learner." She came to the Community Center daily. She was constantly in trouble, and what a mouth! That girl could swear louder and longer than anyone I'd ever known. Almost every day for the first few years of her attendance she would get kicked out for one reason or another. Over time she understood that if we saw her doing something bad she would get sent home. Since she wanted to be with us more than she wanted to be at home she developed a system of doing bad things only when we weren't watching.

One day we discovered that our parking lot was polka-dotted with various forms of feminine hygiene products that used to be stored in the cupboard of our upstairs bathroom. All the kids thought that this was so funny. Who would do such a thing? At first we had no clue. The door going upstairs was always locked. Who had climbed the stairs and gotten into the storage cupboard? Eventually we found out that it was Dolores. She had been hanging out of the upstairs window yelling, "Merry Christmas—it's snowing!" as she threw handfuls of pads and tampons on the kids in the parking lot below.

Dolores had been with us long enough to know that if we saw her doing wrong she would get in trouble, but that knowledge didn't make her well behaved. It only made her behave well in our presence, most of the time.

Behaving well is good, but it is not good enough! The second half of the definition for discipline is, "…to shape their character so they learn how to make healthy choices." The ultimate goal of good discipline is to develop good character within a child. An individual's character holds that person to a higher standard. Character demands choosing what is right instead of choosing what is wrong no matter the circumstances or the degree of peer pressure.

My character is what causes me to tell the cashier he gave me too much change. My character keeps me from stealing when it would be so easy to do because no one is watching. Character restrains me from making an easy choice when I know that in the long run the right choice is the harder one.

Character and discipline are intertwined. Good discipline teaches and promotes good character. A child of good character does not rebel against discipline that is evenhanded, justified, and logical. Character is built up when discipline is applied well. However, when discipline is applied without an understanding of the consequences it is far less effective and the growth of character is inhibited. Discipline and consequences are inseparable.

Consequences and consistency are inseparable, too. Disciplining a child who is not informed of consequences in advance is not productive for the child or the adult. Even as an adult it doesn't feel good when someone yells at me for doing something I didn't know was wrong. I usually go away from an encounter like that questioning their mental stability. Why should it be any different for a child?

Well, it isn't. Discipline that includes known consequences that are applied consistently promotes control and positive learning. The opposite is true, also. Uncontrolled discipline borders on, or leads to abuse, and abuse is wrong. As a society we have agreed upon this. Laws have been passed against abuse. Abusers are separated from the people they could harm and efforts are made to rehabilitate them. The problem is that not everyone agrees on what abuse is and where it comes from. Often it emerges from people who have been abused. These people are broken. In extremes they derive pleasure from making others suffer. In the case of an adult-child relationship, any adult who derives pleasure from making a child suffer is engaging in abuse.

A more common form of "abuse" is seen when a frustrated parent reaches the end of their rope and, without a clear understanding of what to do, lashes out physically or verbally in an effort to take control of a problematic situation and crosses the line into abuse. Discipline that is undecided, uninformed, and uncontrolled can lead in this direction. This type of discipline almost always promotes a rebellious child.

Rules have to be known if they are to be obeyed. Before we posted the rules on the wall of the Community Center we just made them up as we went along. Circumstances dictated our directives. Every day was different and each staff person had the authority to do what seemed best.

I remember one day when one of the kids unrolled an entire roll of toilet paper then tried to flush it all down the toilet. Water was running everywhere. Kids were yelling, splashing, sliding, and pushing while I was trying to mop it all up. At the height of all this chaos, one of the boys said something. I don't even remember what he said, but it was a smart aleck way to get attention from one of the girls.

At that moment I just lost it. I started yelling. I was probably demonstrating abusive behavior — or at least I was heading in that direction. I didn't say anything bad, and I didn't use any words that I had to apologize for. I just overreacted to this young man in a way that I knew was out of line. He hadn't caused the problem. He was just having some fun. But I had taken it personally. I was wrong when I took my frustration out on him.

Sometimes in the heat of the moment we do that with the people around us. We just get fed up with a situation and we explode out of frustration. But if we take the time to develop a discipline plan and make sure that everyone involved knows the details of that plan, the possibility of sliding into abusive behavior becomes more difficult.

To put it another way: Developing a plan of discipline is like tying a knot on the end of your emotional rope. It gives you a little something extra to hold onto at a critical moment. Letting kids know up front what the rules are and what the consequences will be has a positive effect. That knowledge is the knot that keeps you from going too far.

We were getting ready to go on a summer trip from Los Angeles to Mt. Saint Helens, Washington in 1989. The volcano had blown a few years before and we wanted to show our kids an example of "The Power of God." Kids had to earn the right to go, by acquiring points. They received points for school and Bible Club attendance. School attendance alone didn't reward them with enough points; they had to attend Bible Club. Just attending Bible Club would not earn enough points, either; they had to go to school. They also had to memorize thirteen Bible verses.

As the time to leave drew closer the kids got more excited. Every week they made sure they were getting the credits they earned for being at Bible Club, report cards were being turned in to show school attendance, and every day we listened to kids recite their Bible verses.

Antonio, however, was one exception. He was earning points in the areas of Bible Club and school attendance but had not memorized any verses. So I said to him, "Antonio, what choice are you making?"

"John, what do you mean?"

"I mean you have chosen not to say any verses and you can't go on the trip without learning the verses. What is going on? Are you going or not?"

He looked down at his shoes, stood there for a minute then looked up at me through his eyelashes and quietly said, "I don't know yet."

I shrugged, "Okay, it's your choice."

Antonio was one of our best kids. He never caused any trouble and was always willing to help. It would have been a tremendous plus to have him along on the trip. As he walked away I wanted to tell him that no matter what we wanted him to go. Then I remembered it wasn't about what I wanted, it was about what he earned.

A couple days later Antonio came to me when no one was around and shared with me that he couldn't memorize the verses. He told me he had tried, that he had tried really hard. He just couldn't remember the words after he had learned them. Just for the record I knew that this story was not true. This kid knew the words to every song that came on the radio. He knew the oldies, the new songs, and everything in between. This kid had an amazing memory.

So I took him outside to the back steps where we wouldn't be interrupted and gave him the thirteen verses on a piece of paper. "Read me the first verse," I said. So he read it to me.

"Now," I said, "make a song out of it."

"John, I can't do that. I don't know how."

"It's easy, just do it like this."

I started singing the words, putting some rhythm into them, adding a few sound effects like I had heard the rap singers do. It was the most pitiful example of music I had ever heard.

When I was done Antonio was smiling. Not just a normal "Hello, how are you?" smile, but the kind of smile that hurt because he was using muscles in his face he had never used before.

Then it was his turn to make music and my time to smile. He sort of copied what I had done, but the rap sounded much better when he did it.

After going through that first verse a couple times while he was looking at the paper, I had him put it away and recite it from memory. The words were perfect. I didn't like the rap, but the words were perfect. I gave him a big hug and said, "Follow me."

We walked to the wall where the huge chart was hanging that listed the points earned by the kids. I gave him the pen and told him to mark a star in the box by his name for memorizing the first verse. The smile on his face while watching me rap was nothing compared to the one he showed while giving himself credit for memorizing that first Bible verse.

I love telling that story. The joy I felt as I went home that evening came from knowing that I helped Antonio earn something that no one could ever take away from him.

Memorizing a Bible verse may not sound like a very big accomplishment, but for Antonio it was huge.

Now for the rest of the story! The next day I was standing beside the chart listening to verses and marking points when Antonio appeared as next in line. He handed me the sheet from the day before that had all the verses on it. I asked, "What verse are you going to do?" expecting him to repeat just one. He looked at me with another huge grin and said, "All of them." The verses just rolled out of his mouth. As the stars were being recorded on the chart I am not sure who had the bigger smile, me or him.

Here's the moral of this story: I could have given in to my feelings and cheated him out of a tremendous opportunity to realize he was capable of learning. I could have denied him an opportunity of growth on that first day when he had said he wasn't sure that he was going.

Because we took the time to care for this young man, he learned a valuable lesson and earned the right to go. We didn't give him the trip to him—he received it as a reward for his effort.

Antonio had come back to me for two reasons. One was that he really wanted to go on the trip. The other was that he also believed we would be consistent in applying the standards we had set. He knew that if he didn't learn those verses the consequences would be sure: he would be standing watching the bus with his brother and the other kids from the Center inside, pull out of the parking lot for the best ride any of them had ever had in their entire life.

Consequences work. The knowledge of the sure consequence helped Antonio and me come up with an innovative way of getting it done. Consequences make us look closely at our actions or inactions to learn from them, so the next time we do things differently. Consequences are the keys to any effective discipline strategy. Discipline cannot exist without them.

Discipline works best when the consequences of an action come from the knowledge of the boundary. Remember, boundaries are established to define right and wrong. Kids interact with them when they know they exist. The kids may choose to test the boundaries but that is their choice, not mine. When a child steps over the line I don't get mad. I am not and cannot become emotionally invested in whether the kids will follow the rules. I know they won't. It is against human nature to follow all the rules all of the time. When a rule is broken my response must be, "I am sorry that the consequence has to happen, but this was your choice. Maybe next time you can make a better choice."

One Saturday Sheryl and I took a bus load of kids to the beach. Announcements to promote the event had been distributed, permission slips had been signed and collected, and the rules for the day were passed out. Everyone involved knew that the bus was leaving at 9:00 AM sharp. At the appointed time, on the dot, we pulled out.

We had a great time. We played volleyball, bodysurfed in the waves, and built sand castles. Someone even brought a boogie board that everybody tried at least once. We ate sandwiches as we sat on our towels, getting sand in our sandwiches and too much sun on our faces. It was a great day!

As we turned into the Community Center parking lot that evening there were four sad kids sitting on the steps. They knew what time we had planned to return, so I doubt they'd been sitting there all day. Kids piled off the bus as their parents met us. Lots of talking was going on, kids shared about their day, what they had seen, the things they had done, and how much fun they had.

Finally, after things settled down a bit, I walked over to where the four kids were sitting; now looking more mad than sad. "How was your day?" I asked. They all mumbled some version of "terrible." I answered, "Oh. That is too bad. You should have chosen to come to the beach with us."

One of them stood up and with more than a little anger said, "I wanted to, and I was here ready to go, but you left without me!" I responded, "Really, what time did you choose to get here?"

The answer: "Just a little after nine."

"And what time did I say we were going to leave?"

"Nine o'clock, but you knew I was coming, so you could have waited."

I chose my next words carefully, "Yes, we could have chosen to wait. But then I would have been insulting everyone who had chosen to get here on time. And the next time I'd choose to say we are leaving at nine, who would believe me?"

"But I didn't get to go, and I was looking forward to going!"

"Yes, I understand that. And I was looking forward to having you go with us. When we do this again maybe you'll make the choice to be on time, and join us." I was not too amazed that from that time on those four kids were early to every event, every time we went anywhere.

It is just that easy. A power struggle no longer positions their wills against my will. In fact I am not the one who is disciplining them; rather, their choices of actions earn the consequences they endure.

11

Cornerstone Number Three — Freedom

As we progressed, Sheryl and I looked for signs and signals that would indicate success or failure. We continually endeavored to identify the Four Core Needs and use them to understand the children and the motives behind their actions. At the same time we employed Cornerstone Number One—Empowerment, and Cornerstone Number Two—Responsibility, to help our kids build better lives. The results we saw from our efforts appeared to be very good.

- As our discipline techniques improved our kids became more deliberate and less emotionally driven in their choices.

- As we became more consistent in our behaviors our kids began to respect and honor the boundaries we laid down.
- We watched as more and more of our kids chose to stay in school.
- We saw gang involvement go down in the families with whom we were involved.

Some years later I was having lunch with a person who also worked with at- risk kids. She knew our program well and suggested a way to make what we were doing even more effective. She thought there was a gap in the way the cornerstones of Life Is Full of Choices dealt with the past experiences of our kids. She pointed out that the displays of anger or frustration of today were often the products of negative circumstances that had occurred before. The residual feelings from those circumstances needed to be dealt with. Without dealing with them there could be little chance or opportunity for diffusing the anger and mitigating the frustration.

We considered her comments carefully. We prayed a lot and talked with our kids about it. We decided to add another cornerstone. This one would combine the ideas of freedom from the past and control of the future.

Cornerstone Number One had said:

> *Life is full of choices,*
> *and the choices I make today*
> *will determine the qualities of my life*
> *both now and in the future.*

Cornerstone Number Two had said:

> *Life is full of choices,*
> *and the choices I make today*
> *can affect the circumstances of my life*
> *and other people's lives*
> *both now and in the future.*

We had reviewed Cornerstone Number One and Cornerstone Number Two and considered that if we could improve the overall concept we would help our kids understand and then believe three important truths:

1. I have choices.
2. My choices have a lasting influence on me and those around me.
3. I am in control of the qualities of my life.

With control comes responsibility, of course, but we didn't see a direct connection in the first two cornerstones between the way my life is today and the responsibility I have for how I live it.

So we created Cornerstone Number Three to provide that new context. We wanted to confront the thought pattern of, "I didn't make a lot of the choices when I was young so I am not responsible for the way I am today." Even though the idea of responsibility was already addressed in Cornerstone Number One and Cornerstone Number Two we decided a more obvious connection was necessary.

We designed Cornerstone Number Three. It said:

Life is full of choices,
and even though I have not chosen
all the circumstances of my life,
I alone determine its qualities, because
life is full of choices,
and the choices I make today
will determine the qualities of my life
both now and in the future.

Freedom from the past is found in Cornerstone Number Three. Within it the victim mentality that our kids had acquired would have the chance of being brought out into the open, dealt with, and removed from their life.

Let me personalize it. Circumstances can only determine the qualities of my life when I allow them to. When I choose to let my circumstances determine the qualities of my life, those circumstances or their effects become *my* choices. They are not the result of what someone else has done to me. At one and the same time I cannot control the qualities of my life and blame someone else for who I am now or the person I become.

The people I blame and the excuses I come up with only separate me from my responsibility for the content of my life. It is *my* life. The person I am on the inside is demonstrated on the outside by the choices I make. When I understand that I am ultimately in control of the qualities of my life only then can I start to make the changes I want to make in order to become the person I desire to be. It is my life, and it is my life now.

Sarah was a young lady who blamed her mother for the ugly apartment they lived in, her rotten school, and their dangerous neighborhood. But most of all Sarah didn't like that her mother's sewing job kept her away from the house for twelve hours a day, six days a week. Sarah was angry about her circumstances. She was mad at everyone and constantly got into trouble because of her poor attitude. She had no control over her mother's job. Her mother was just glad to even have a job that paid the bills and allowed them to live in an apartment instead of on the street. But Sarah only saw that her mother was gone when Sarah came home from school. Sarah had choices. She could choose to be mad at her mother for being gone and become an angry person, or she could choose to be glad that her mother had a job and become a grateful person.

In another instance a kid named Julio was talking to Roberto, and said something about Roberto coming from a certain town in Mexico. That comment brought up emotions from Roberto's past when he was put down for being a "wetback." Without examining where those emotions were coming from Roberto just reacted by hitting Julio.

We talked about this later. We were sitting at a table playing a game and I asked Roberto what had happened. Notice I didn't ask him why he had hit Julio. I simply asked what had happened. Roberto said, "He made me mad." Roberto chose to believe that Julio had control of him and could make him mad. The reality was that Roberto gave Julio power over him by choosing to react in anger.

Here's the point: The qualities of my life are not determined by my education, income, language, birth family, neighborhood, or ethnicity. The qualities present in my life are determined by my choices *and only by my choices*. If someone says a kid is stupid that child begins to act stupid only when the kid chooses to believe they are stupid. At that point they choose to give up control of their life to someone else, they quit studying, drop out of school, join a gang, and start acting stupid because they have chosen that path for themselves.

The fundamental reality of life found in Cornerstone Number Three is this: My circumstances can never determine the qualities of my life unless I choose to allow them to.

> My circumstances can never determine the qualities of my life unless I choose to allow them to.

Cornerstone Number Three takes us back to where we started. No one determines the qualities of my life for me. If I am dissatisfied with the qualities of my life right now I can improve it by making different choices, because "Life is full of choices, and the choices I make today will determine the qualities of my life both now and in the future."

The qualities of my life are determined by the choices I make. These choices affect all the relationships I have, including those with my family, social networks, and people I work with. My choices even affect my relationship to God. That relationship is the most important one of all. When I choose to enter that relationship the person I become can never be taken from me in this life or eternity. That is a good choice and a great result.

12

Choices or Decisions

Presenting the truths of the Three Cornerstones to our Community Center children became matters of choice of vocabulary and consistent action. We chose to follow up our words with actions that could be counted on. We proved that when we said we would do something, we would do it.

We chose to never use the word *decision* when we were dealing with a child's behavior. Instead, we used the word *choice*. By talking to our children about their choices instead of their decisions we brought a new understanding of their responsibilities for the actions they chose.

A decision is a mental process. A choice precedes an

action. Here are examples: Let's say I need money so I decide
to rob a bank. When I get to the bank there's an armed guard
in the parking lot so I choose to change my mind. Or, I decide
to invite Jackie to the dance. When I see her at school her
leg is in a cast so I choose to ask Sally, instead. I decide to
vote for George Smith for Governor. As I drive to my polling
place I hear him on the radio saying that he will give the state
employees a raise. I know this action will raise my taxes, so I
choose to vote for David Jones, instead. There is a great deal
of difference between choice and decision.

When a child didn't do his homework and explained it to
me with the phrase, "I decided I didn't want to do it because it
was just busy work," I would respond with, "I don't care what
you decided; you don't get the reward because you chose not
to do your homework. Your decision was irrelevant. What
you decided became irrelevant when you chose to act. Until
that moment you were fine. It was your choice that got you
in trouble, not your decision."

Once a person has the facts about choices and understands
the role that choices play in the process of making their
decisions become reality, their decisions may not sound as
good as they first appeared. I've participated in a variation of
a conversation hundreds of times. It usually goes like this:

He says, "I have decided I want to go to Harvard." I say,

"That is great. Now what choices are you going to do to make that decision a reality?"

"I don't understand."

"To be accepted into Harvard you need to have at least a 3.8 GPA and be involved in lots of extra curricular activities. What is your GPA?"

"2.4"

"To bring it up to 3.8 in two years you will need to get a tutor and study twice as long every night. Are you willing to do that in order to go to Harvard?"

"What kind of GPA do I need to get into UCLA?"

You don't get put in jail for thinking you will rob a bank, and you don't get in trouble for thinking of not doing your homework. You only get in trouble when the thought, or decision, becomes a choice and then an action.

We designed specific Standards of Behavior, printed them on poster board, and hung them on the walls. Those standards described behaviors that were acceptable and behaviors that were not.

Some of those standards and consequences were these:

Choice	Consequence
Fighting	Go home for today
Sharing	Gain $1.00
Swearing	Lose $1.00
Praising another kid	Gain $1.00
Throwing things in the Center	Lose $1.00
Clean up someone else's mess	Gain $1.00

If the standard was "No Swearing" and the consequence was having $1.00 taken away we enforced the consequence when one of our kids swore. There was no discussion, no bargaining, and no "grace." The consequence just happened. We chose never to accept excuses for behavior. "I forgot" didn't matter, either. What they did was totally up to them. They made the choices, they experienced the consequences.

Sheryl and I decided that if we were going to strive to be consistent we had to choose to be consistent in our all of our actions, not just in our promises, but in every way we could. We chose to never negotiate over a boundary or a consequence. If we said we were going to leave at 9:00 AM and be back before 4:00 PM we had to be consistent on both ends. The van had to drive out of the driveway before the clock reached 9:01 AM and we had to be back—no matter what—before 4:00 PM.

We took a group of kids to the mall. Once they were there the kids could go anywhere they wanted but they had to be at the food court at 8:30 PM so we could load up and arrive home by 9:30 PM. A small group of kids thought it would be great sport to make us late. They just didn't show up and we couldn't find them when it came time to leave. After not being allowed to go on the next few trips, they decided the momentary fun wasn't worth suffering the consequence of watching the group leave while they stayed behind.

After about six months of not going on outings, I invited these same kids to go with me to the store to buy some things for a Friday Night Dinner. As we left the Community Center I told them this was a test and that if they passed the test they would be able to go on the next outing. If they didn't pass, another six months of watching and waving goodbye was in store. They chose to abide by the rules and were happily reinstated to the trip list.

We didn't try to make the kids behave in a certain way. We allowed the choices they made to result in consequences that had already been decided. They experienced the truth that their choices came with consequences. They discovered that in real life they either enjoyed positive rewards or negative results.

If they said "please" they received $1.00; if they swore,

$1.00 was taken away. When playing a game, if they cheated they lost $1.00; if they encouraged another kid they received $1.00. If they shared paper, pencils, or toys with the person sitting next to them they received $1.00. This was real life.

Here's the point: In behavioral issues start with the little things and always reward behaviors you want to encourage. Rewarded behaviors will be repeated. Pretty soon these can become a welcome habit.

We saw a paradigm shift in the behavior of our kids as they began to see life as a series of choices to be dealt with instead of a collection of random events. Their understanding and changed behaviors were in direct proportion to our willingness to be consistent in our words and actions. When we were consistent in rewarding kids who said "please" very soon more kids were saying "please." When we forgot to reward their "please" pretty soon kids were not saying it any more.

> Their understanding and changed behaviors were in direct proportion to our willingness to be consistent in our words and actions.

We discovered that every word coming out of our mouths was a contract with a child. Before we made the contract (by opening our mouth) we had to choose if we really wanted to make that contract. If we weren't willing to follow through with what we were going to say, then we should not say it. Our actions had to follow our words because "actions speak louder than words."

> Every word coming out of our mouths was a contract with a child.

13

When, Where, and How

The purpose of this book is to teach parents, guardians, and caregivers how to help kids grow into responsible adults. Kids mature in different areas of their lives at the same time. They grow emotionally, mentally, physically, socially, and spiritually.

We worked in all of those areas at the Community Center. We created a balanced environment. We helped them mature emotionally, meeting their Four Core Needs. We provided homework time with our kids to help them grow mentally. We set aside a time of recreation every day to help them develop physically. We monitored their interaction with other kids to help advance their sense of social well-being, using the Three Cornerstones. We included Bible Club in our weekly activities because we were convinced that spiritual development was vital, too, if not foundational to all sustained success. As missionaries it was important for us to have this Christian focus.

"Life Is Full of Choices" is not a Christian concept. At its center it is just common sense. We used the concept to pave the way for Christian thought and action. The same concept can be used by any organization to advance their agenda, even by a gang to promote social dysfunction and lawlessness. It's all about motive and means. The bottom line is this: Life is all about choices. We wanted our kids to make good ones.

When an adult chooses to develop a healthy relationship with a child, that relationship provides a model that can help grow an emotionally strong and balanced kid. The kid learns that they can pattern their life after the adult who has shown them the way. The adult may be a parent, grandparent, aunt or uncle, teacher, Sunday school teacher, neighbor, or Boy Scout leader. The title doesn't matter. That person must be an adult who is willing to put valiant effort into building a right relationship.

A relationship of quality is not constructed overnight. It's a long term commitment. It's doing the best we can to help them grow. It's making sure we consistently show them the right paths to follow as they mature. While we strive to do our best we always remember that their choices are always their choices. We are not taking responsibility for their choices or feeling responsible for the consequences that naturally follow those choices.

We will look at *when, where,* and *how* the cornerstones were used to give our kids a clear picture of the world around them. In *Parenting from the Top of the Mountain,* the second book in the *Life Is Full of Choices Series,* giving them this vantage point is explained fully.

When is easy. The simple answer is, all the time. We would talk about their choices because we cared enough to pay attention to the kids, spending time with them and interacting with them. However, kids do not, or may not learn on our time schedule. Teachable moments happen when the students are ready. Those moments almost always would occur when we were already doing something with them. We'd look for the teachable moments in our interactions with them. When we discovered the right time we would strive to reinforce the concept of choices. We wanted to be ready to direct them back to the truth of making good choices.

If kids were fighting, instead of asking, "Why are you fighting?" we would ask, "What choice are you making?" If they considered the question and answered it, they understood they had already chosen a prearranged consequence for their actions. When kids were being rewarded, instead of saying to them, "You shared the ball when you were playing basketball," we told them, "You made a good choice to share the ball while paying basketball." When we talked about someone else's behavior we would say, "What choice did he make?" We would follow this comment with, "What other choice could he have made?" and "What choice would you have made?"

I came to the conclusion that for the Three Cornerstones to be effective, I wanted to talk about choices enough so that when I would see one of the children acting up I could hold up my hand in the shape of a "C" and they would know exactly what I meant. I knew I was on the right track when children started hearing "Life is full of choices" in their head because of my hand signal and started to think about what they were doing.

Where is also not difficult to explain. The simple answer is, everywhere. We should be talking about choices on the playground, in the kitchen, doing devotions, riding in the car, and at the store. No matter where we were, when we saw an opportunity that location became the perfect place to talk about choices. We didn't wait until we were in a quiet place where we had their total attention. We didn't wait until we were alone so we wouldn't embarrass them or us.

Once in a while, to avoid a confrontation I would say to a kid, "When we get back to the car we are going to talk about this." That put a bookmark in their memory that we could access later.

We would not talk about their poor choices just to embarrass them, but we would not avoid talking about poor choices if it might embarrass them. We strove to always remember that this process was about growing kids. It was about being consistent with them, not about being their friend. Building a relationship was a whole different process than becoming a friend. We wanted a relationship that lasted beyond friendship.

Building a relationship is a whole different process than becoming a friend.

How is the method, the process of making the *when* and *where* concrete. This is the fun part. Sheryl and I used Bible Club gatherings as opportunities for kids to memorize scripture and tell Bible stories to them. We related the Bible stories to illustrate choices, and we memorized scripture that had been paraphrased to show how choices affected outcomes.

Using the concept of choices like this, John 3:16 would say: "For God chose to love the world so much that He chose to give His only Son, so that everyone who chooses to believe in Him won't be lost but will be choosing to have life that lasts forever." Romans 12:1 would become: "So, brothers and sisters, because of what God has done for us, I encourage you to choose to give your bodies as a gift that is holy and pleasing to God. This is the least you should choose to do." Revelation 3:20 would read: "Look! I'm choosing to stand at the door and knock. If anyone chooses to hear my voice and chooses to open the door, I will choose to come in and be with him, and we will have dinner together."

Whether the choice was positive or negative didn't matter. Noah chose to build the ark, David chose to fight Goliath, and Jesus chose to die on the cross. Adam chose to eat the fruit, David chose to have Uria killed, and Judas chose to betray Jesus.

It got really exciting when we applied the Four Core Needs and the Three Cornerstones together. When we saw a child acting as if he wanted some affection we gave him a hug, or a pat, or something that would meet his need for affection, then we would talk to him about the choice he was making to ask for affection. That conversation would often go like this:

During the hug I would say, "It is really good to see you today."

He would often say something profound like "Yeah."

Then I would ask him, "Do you like being here, playing games, getting some hugs from us?"

Another profound response: "Yeah."

"You know, when I was your age, I didn't have place to go after school. I came home to an empty house. Sometimes it was pretty lonely. I am glad that we can be here for you and I am glad that you are making the choice to be here with us so we can play some games and have fun together."

"Yeah, me, too."

I had just used Cornerstone Number One — Empowerment to reinforce my commitment to help him meet his need for affection. He may have not known of his core need or what it was called but he did know that he enjoyed being at the Community Center. I knew that after I reinforced my commitment he would probably be back tomorrow instead of out on the street.

Now clearly, not everyone gets hugs. Some kids get a high five, others get patted on the shoulder, and other kids receive time playing a game or working on homework. The important thing was to let the child know that what they were feeling was normal. After all, I felt it when I was his age, and we were there to help because we had been there, too, and because we cared.

Kids ask for affection in many ways. Sometimes their request is as simple arms outstretched. Sometimes it is seen as a scowl or a pout, and sometimes the kid indicates it by his demeanor. It may be observed when they just walk through the door. You might see that trouble is in store by the gait, the attitude, or simply the way they were talking. I may not know what I am observing but when I would see the behaviors I would go up to them and start asking questions. Eventually, if the child chose to answer, we would get to the bottom of what was going on. Usually it was the need for affection. Sometimes they just needed to be reassured that the boundaries were still in place but most often affection was at the core of their deficiency.

The answer I was looking for as I asked questions was something that would start with, "I don't know. I just feel _____." You can fill in the blank. If the feeling was mad, sad, angry, all alone, fed up, ignored, confused, or any other emotionally descriptive word or phrase I would respond with "Oh, okay. I understand. Come with me and let's _____." Again you can fill in the blank.

At that point I might invite him to play a game with me, or unload the van, or stack some boxes in the storage room, or start dinner for the group. The task didn't matter. The important part was hearing what he was feeling, accepting it as normal, and then spending time doing something together. I could then say, "It really is good to see you today." "Do you like being able to be here with us?"

If a child expressed a need for affection one day, I would try to meet them at the door the following day with a handshake, a pat on the back, or a hug—just something to recognize that they were here and that I was glad to see them here. Often I would include the statement, "I am glad that you chose to be here today so I could spend time with you. Thank you."

It was not hard to do this. I understood that I was making a deposit into a core needs bank account. I was making that deposit in relation to a choice they had made. Over time the kids would start to recognize that they were making the choice to feel good by coming to the Community Center.

As time went on, when they were a little more advanced, we could sit down and talk about how Cornerstone Number One—Empowerment meant that their choice to be at the Community Center allowed us to meet their need for affection. They would begin to understand that their choice to be here was better than the choice to join a gang, rob the grocery store, create a pattern of negative behavior, and spend half their life in jail.

When a child wanted to know if the boundaries were still in place they usually acted more defiant and more demanding. Typical comments sounded like this: "What will you do if I don't?" or, "You can't make me!" and "So what! What are you going to do about it?" Our first response would always be, "What is the rule?" I would always ask that question with my arm pointing at the spot where the rules were written on the wall so there would be no confusion. I would identify the boundary for them.

Remember, a boundary is not a discussion point, nor is it the time for a power struggle between a child and me. The boundary is because it is. There is no leeway, no negotiation, and no flexibility.

When the kid understood the boundary my next question was, "Now that you know what the rule is, what choice you are going to make?"

"What do you mean?"

"Well, your choice to stick within the boundary or step over the line will have an effect on your life. You can choose to stay here and play and have fun, or you can choose to go home. What choice are you going to make?"

Usually all they wanted to know was whether I would carry though on enforcing a boundary. With my question I would put the responsibility back on them, where it belonged. It was their choice and they would enjoy whatever consequences they earned. "Because, you know, life is full of choices, and the choices you make today will determine the qualities of your life, both now and in the future."

If there was a small group and one kid asked the question

the answer would be the same, but I would use Cornerstone Number Two—Responsibility to remind all of them that responsibility would be shared. If one person stepped over the line and I saw that other kids were daring him to do so, then all of them would be looking at the consequence. "Because, you know, life is full of choices, and the choices you make today can affect the circumstances of your life and other people's lives, both now and in the future."

A cry for consistency would often start with, "Why?" Or, "That's not fair!" Those words were usually used in one of two situations. The first one was when I had not been consistent and the kids were feeling unsure. Where they had been used to having an anchor to support them in a turbulent world my inconsistent response to some situation had left them feeling ill at ease. The other time was when their life was in turmoil and they were looking for reassurance within our structure. Often that assurance was needed after I had made a mistake. If I had caused a problem, I needed to fix it. I had to figure out what I had done that was inconsistent with our procedures. That was not too difficult because generally there were twenty kids telling me what I had done wrong. I needed to work with the kid to whom I had given the wrong answer, the wrong consequence, or the wrong reward. Whatever I had done, I needed to make it right.

Then I had to offer an apology to the group. It was a recommitment on my part to abide by the rules. Usually I also needed to thank the kids for calling to my attention that I had slipped up. It was difficult when I'd realize that my choice of inconsistency affected the circumstances of my life and other people's lives. If I had broken trust with my kids then I had to start rebuilding it again.

When a child felt a need for reassurance it often represented a desire to know that the boundaries were still in place. What they really wanted was to feel secure that a consequence would come if a boundary was crossed. If a kid knew something was going on in their life that might cause them to feel insecure, the important action we the caregivers could take was to ask them what the rules were. We had to get them to tell us. This action had more power when they heard their own voice say it than when they heard us tell them.

Once they started telling us the boundaries we could say, "Okay. So what happens if you cross the boundaries?" Then we would wait for them to tell us what the consequences would be. Then we might say, "Very good. So what do you want to do today?" While engaged in an activity with them we could talk about how someone else had made poor choices and how those choices affected their circumstances, explaining that those negative choices did not have to determine who they were. Then we would start listing the characteristics about them that we liked. As we did this we reinforced our commitment to uphold the boundary while we genuinely turned into a cheerleader and spent time encouraging them.

We learned to spot the signals. When a child felt the need for discipline sometimes they were really asking if we cared about them. It was easy to tell the difference. If they were looking for affirmation they would approach the boundary, whatever it was, look at us and then step over the line — but only just a little. All they wanted was to see if we were paying attention and would respond. After we responded we would make sure to give them the affection they were asking for.

When a child was asking for discipline we needed to give them discipline. We didn't talk about discipline — we simply gave it to them. Remember, actions speak louder than words. At home if the rule was "No Throwing Toys in the House" and my seven year old picked up a ball and looked at me, I'd already figured out what was going to happen. When he threw the ball it didn't matter how far it would go. What mattered was that he was asking, "Am I important enough to you for you to put down your book and deal with me?"

If the child was not asking for affirmation he would not look at us. He simply didn't care. He just wanted to throw the ball. This is a different situation, but we would deal with it in the same way. The kid was asking for discipline. We needed to give him discipline.

After the discipline had been administered, when the kid had had his time out, or the TV has been turned off for the rest of the afternoon, we could start to play a game with him.   While playing the game we could ask a question such as, "What choice have you made today that is affecting the circumstances of your life right now?" Or, "If you had to do it over again what different choice would you make so the circumstances in your life would be better right now?"

When he would come to us to ask if he could watch whatever his favorite afternoon TV program was, we could say, "I would love for you to be able to watch that program — but it appears that you made a choice today to throw the ball in the house. Is it okay to throw the ball in the house?"

"No."

"What happens when you throw the ball in the house?"

"I don't get to watch TV for the rest of the afternoon."

"Can I let you watch your show?"

"Yes. You can if you want."

"No, I can't, because the rules say I can't. It is not up to me. This choice was up to you."

The bottom line was that we were not punishing the child for breaking the rules. By throwing the ball he had chosen not to watch TV.

At the Community Center when a child complained about the circumstances of life that were beyond his or our control, such as the neighborhood in which they lived, the school they attended, the teacher they had for math, sharing their room with a younger brother, the kind of car the parents drove, that child was really asking for a life lesson. He would be saying, "Life is not fair and I need some help in understanding it."

This would become a perfect time to remember and restate Cornerstone Number Three — Freedom. After we would agree with him by saying, "Yes, life is not fair..." then we would start the conversation about how we cannot control everything and we aren't necessarily in charge of what we have or don't have. We could say, "Sure, we'd love to have a bigger house, have a nicer math teacher, and live closer to Grandma. While it is okay to wish for a change it is not healthy to spend your time complaining about something you can't change. If all you do is complain you'll become bitter and defeated. So, instead, you should ask: 'What can I choose to do, to make this situation better?'" At that point a child would start to learn that it is about their attitude or paradigm, that they possessed the freedom to choose now. They would learn they were free to change their attitude.

Every time my life touched a child's life I could choose to talk about the choices I have made and the consequences that have resulted from those choices. I could also choose to talk about the choices they are making and the consequences that have resulted or will result. This would not be a momentary teaching topic in an otherwise busy day. "Choices" would become the foundation, the focal point for everything we would say and do with our kids.

The pronouns in the Three Cornerstones are personal — the choices *I* make, and the qualities of *my* life. This focus was created deliberately. It doesn't do any good to talk about "they" and "theirs" when "they" are not present. Besides, other's choices don't determine anything for me. Only my choices do.

It's a long term process for a person to change their paradigm after exposure to the truths of the Three Cornerstones. It is not a quick fix. It takes continual reinforcement. We tried to focus every discussion onto the choices our kids were making and in this way we helped them move away from an entitlement mentality toward the responsibility of making healthier choices for themselves.

We used the Three Cornerstones as a tool to start a dialogue that brought to light the choices our kids were making. We openly discussed how their choices determined the qualities of their lives at that moment and into the future.

In the end, however, it was not the application of the Three Cornerstones or meeting their Four Core Needs that changed our kids. Our process included these truths, but it was much more. Ministry from a Christian worldview is driven by the belief that God is the One who changes lives. We believed and taught that God was real and cared enough about us to bring us face to face with Jesus. In this encounter each person has the choice to accept Him as Savior. We shared that when Jesus resides at the center of my life He starts the process of changing me from the inside out. But accepting Jesus as my Savior and letting Him into my life is a choice I have to make. We reaffirmed this truth: "Life is full of choices, and the choices I make today will determine the qualities of my life both now and in the future."

14

Where Are They Now?

Some stories have happy endings, some do not. Walt Disney built an empire on fantasy, saving Bambi from the forest fire and Cinderella from her wicked stepsisters. Such endings, however, do not represent real life.

I wish I could tell you that all of our kid's stories ended happily but that would not be true. Some kids did well, remained in school, stayed out of gangs, and are doing okay. Other kids made poor choices that resulted in their lives becoming hard, even cruel. And other kids, for a variety of reasons, just disappeared. Most of these we never heard from again.

Josiah

As I tell the story of Josiah let me start with some general information that may not be as obvious as it should be. The truth and effectiveness of Life Is Full of Choices, the Three Cornerstones, and the Four Core Needs are in no way affected by race, culture, or education. Choices are the reality of life for every person. Everyone makes them and all people are affected by them. My choices define who I am. My choices illustrate to others what is important to me. My choices determine the course of my life. My choices may affect you. My choices are impacted by my own core needs and my own understanding of the cornerstones.

There is much being said these days about race and the racial divide. A young African American man named Josiah came to the Community Center. He found out about us at school through one of our regular kids. Josiah was a good kid. He was articulate, smart, and fun to be around. He was also one of the only African Americans at the Center. Almost everyone involved in our Community Center program was Hispanic.

The inner city is highly segregated. Most people groups choose to live within their own culture. They are more comfortable with those who speak the same language, who share the same heritage and ethnicity. But even within similar cultures segregation exists. One of the reasons the churches around us did not want our kids to be included in their activities was because their kids were primarily Central American and our kids were Mexican.

Racial prejudice comes in all shapes and sizes, colors and flavors, of course. We never tolerated racial prejudice in our family, and since we were the outsiders in East Los Angeles, we didn't tolerate it at the Community Center, either.

One day Josiah walked through the front door and I could tell that something was wrong. It looked like he was about to explode. I could see it in the way he was walking, talking, and interacting with the other kids. I took him aside and asked, "How was your day?"

He gave me the normal teenage, "Fine."

I looked at him and said, "Something is the matter. It looks like you are ready to hit someone or start yelling or something like that. You know those actions will get you in trouble. Now you can choose to talk to me about what is going on or you can wait and eventually self destruct. It's your choice. What do you want to do?"

He chose to talk. He told me about how his math teacher had declared his chance of success in life at near zero because of his race and his economic situation. Actually the teacher didn't quite say it that way. The expressions the teacher used were crude and totally inappropriate for anyone, let alone a thirteen year old in front of his class at school.

Josiah looked at me with some of the biggest eyes I have ever seen filled with the most hurt I had ever witnessed. He said, "What can I do? That teacher will never give me an even break. I am going to fail his class because of his feeling about who I am and what I am capable of."

As I sat there I asked myself, "What am I doing here? What can I say that will make any difference to this kid? How can I even begin to understand what he is feeling?" Then in a moment of clarity the principles of Life Is Full of Choices took over. I asked him, "What do you want to do?" His answer: "I want to go get a gun from my brother and shoot him in the head."

I responded, "You could do that, but then you would prove that the teacher was right. Your choice to react in anger would make what he said about you come true. Do you want his words to have that much power over you? Or do you want to prove him wrong?"

"But he said I was ….."

"I know what he chose to say. But that is not the issue. His choice is irrelevant. The important part is the choice you will make about your future. Do you want to get elected to the

School Board and be able to decide if people like him should teach kids math, or do you want to spend the next twenty years in jail?"

We talked about how that one teacher's statement could influence his whole life, but that it didn't have to. Josiah could choose to let it go. He could choose to rise above what that teacher thought of him and his race and become a better person than he was now and a better man than the teacher would ever be.

That day Josiah made the choice to use racism as a stepping stool to bigger and better things. He chose well. He replaced hate and self destruction with a choice to improve himself.

He moved away shortly after that and we lost track of him. The kids told us that he moved out of the neighborhood because of the gang his brother was in. The next year that math teacher's contract was not renewed.

Donna

Donna was probably the worst behaved kid we ever tried to work with. She had a foul mouth, she was emotionally damaged, and she was failing in school. Most of the time, she didn't even bother to go to school. When she attended class she just got into trouble. By not going to school she stayed out of trouble and her teachers were glad she wasn't there.

As a fifth grader she played around on the fringes of a gang. Her young life was beginning to go down the wrong direction. One day she came to the Community Center with a little box under one arm. She asked, "Want to see something?"

"Sure," I said. "What do you have?"

She lifted the lid to show me the scrawniest, smallest bird I had ever seen. There was no way that bird was going to make it; it probably would not live through the night. She told me the story about how the bird had fallen from the tree and how she had waited to see if the mom would show up. It didn't, so Donna had a pet. She was going to feed it, teach it how to fly, and when it was big enough she would release it.

Right about then Sheryl got involved with lots of encouragement and helpful hints about how the bird needed to be kept warm and what it needed to eat. Donna was out the door to find a hot water bottle and some worms.

The next day Donna was back and the bird actually looked a little better. To hear her talk about that bird, it was the best thing in her life. She would set her alarm to wake up every two hours all night long. She would change the water in the water bottle, feed him a worm, then wait for the alarm to go off again and repeat the process. With six people living in a one bedroom apartment I'm not sure how the rest of the family survived those nights of constant bird care.

For the next few weeks I never saw Donna without that box. Finally, one day, Donna announced it was time to let Herman go. Quite a crowd gathered on the front steps to watch this event. Donna nudged Herman out of the box and onto the railing. She kept nudging him toward the end of the railing. Eventually Herman ran out of railing and learned to fly.

Her choice to adopt that bird changed Donna's life. She is now living with her husband and four kids away from Los Angeles. She chose to live away from the rest of her family because of the gangs and violence. She didn't want that environment for her kids. We hear from her every few weeks.

The choice she made to care for another creature changed her. Now her care extends to her family. We also benefit from the positive choice she made. It is such a good feeling to hear her words, "How can I pray for you?"

Phillip

When we took eighteen kids from Los Angeles, California to Mt. Saint Helens, Washington for a summer trip in 1989, we gave everyone who went with us a job to do. Some were responsible for setting up, others for cleaning up, still others for packing or unpacking. Even with a small group of kids we had lots of jobs that had to be done.

The best job any kid could get was the one to keep everyone awake during the day. We passed out squirt guns and if someone started dozing off it was their job to keep them awake. By doing this we hoped that when night came and the adults needed to sleep the kids would be tired enough so we could all rest in peace.

We had a blast. We waded in the headwaters of the Sacramento River. We water-skied on the Willamette River, swam in the Pacific Ocean on the Oregon Coast, and spent three nights in the California Redwoods sleeping in the open on a tarp where the lowest branches were 200 feet over our heads.

While on that trip we focused our devotional times on the Cornerstones of Life Is Full of Choices. One of our kids was Phillip and he got it! Phillip was responsible for two of the more important jobs. Cleaning up after we stopped for lunch was his area of responsibility. We always wanted to leave the rest area or park cleaner than it was when we arrived. Making sure things were packed on top of the bus in an orderly fashion so we didn't loose anything as we were driving down the road, was his other responsibility. While he led these activities he would talk to some of the younger kids working with him about the choices they were making.

Phillip would ask, "What kind of choice is that to put...?" Or, "When you walk over in that direction and avoid all this stuff right here, are you making that choice on purpose?" We would hear him compliment them, "Good choice to set those bags in a line on the rack on top of the bus. That way the wind will not blow them off!" When we heard him using the word *choices* instead of just randomly talking about what was happening we knew he was seeing the value of Life Is Full of Choices in his own life.

After we returned to Los Angeles Phillip came to me and mentioned that he had developed a little problem. I inquired, "What kind of problem?" Phillip said, "I don't have any credits toward graduation." I was amazed. "You are going into your junior year of High School. How could you not have any credits toward graduation?"

"Well, most of the time if you show up once in a while, and especially on the last day of school, they just promote you to the next grade."

"So what keeps you from going to school?"

"Math."

"Math?"

"Yeah, I don't like math. So whenever I can I just skip school."

This was an opportunity. I questioned, "So if we could help you with math, you think you would go to school more often?"

"Yeah, the rest of it is okay. I just don't understand most of what they are talking about when it comes to math."

"Okay. It is July. We will find you a tutor and you will spend two hours every day for the next four weeks learning math. Agreed?"

Phillip nodded. This arrangement worked out perfectly because for the next four weeks a young lady by the name of Jennifer, a college summer intern, was working with us. Jennifer was a math major. She met with Phillip each day of the week for the next month. By the time she left to go back to Asbury College she told us that he was doing quite well.

Phillip started going to school. He would bring his report cards and we watched his grades go from "D's" and "F's" to "C's" and "B's" the next year. At the end of that year we had a lot to celebrate when he passed all his classes, including algebra. Fast food might not seem like much of a celebration but his brother and I shared in his accomplishment by devouring hamburgers and fries with him.

Little by little we saw a change in Phillip's attitude. While we knew he possessed leadership skills, there had always been an uncertainty when he tried to lead. Now he showed confidence. When he identified something that needed to be done he was much more likely to grab a couple kids and get the job done by working with them.

We kept track of his attendance the next year through weekly reports from his teachers but didn't see his grades until the last week of school. One day I was working on our van in the parking lot and Phillip walked up. He said, "John, I have something to show you." As I turned around I saw he was standing with one arm behind his back. He waited until he had my full attention and then with a flourish proclaimed, "Tah-Dah!" and brought his arm around in front of his chest.

In his hand he held an Honor Roll Certificate that had been presented to Phillip Ramos. This young man had ended his senior year of High School with his name on the Honor Roll! Celebrations galore: at the Community Center, with his family, and even a private one with just him, Sheryl, and me.

No one from his family had ever appeared on an Honor Roll. No one from his family had ever finished High School. And we were even more excited fourteen months later when he graduated from High School after attending an Adult Education program.

Those were special days for him and his family. He had paved the way of success for himself and inspired others.

In the years that followed two of his younger brothers also graduated from High School. Now Phillip holds a good job as head of a bank transportation department in Southern California. Phillip: well done.

Jacob

Jacob was riding in the van with us 1994 when we returned from a week of fun at Yosemite National Park. We had swum in the rivers, hiked the trails, rappelled down some rocks, and experienced what life can be when you are not running away from gang members or dodging their bullets.

After driving for most of the day through the California desert we stopped at a rest area on the top of the grapevine. This familiar stop is located along Interstate 5 as the road winds through the mountains separating Kern County from Los Angeles County.

Our van was old and beat up. We had inherited it from someone who thought the vehicle wasn't worth trading in on a new car. It did not have air conditioning. It was temperamental. We had given this old van a name: Flattery. Because, as we all know, Flattery will get you nowhere.

By the time we reached the rest stop it was evening. Our travel day had been excessively warm. It was cooler on the grass outside than it was inside the van so everyone wanted to get out.

Get a visual on this. We had been traveling all day with a group of teenagers in a hot van and we finally had arrived at a good spot to let them get out so they could run around, burn some of their surplus energy, and cool off. I announced, "You have a half an hour to scream, jump, and run then we are back on the road." The kids took advantage of that!

Half an hour later we collected everyone back into the van and I reached down to turn the ignition key. Nothing happened. Well, okay—it was probably nothing to worry about. This had happened before. In fact, I had even taken the van to a mechanic at one point to evaluate the ignition problem and he had informed me that the starter and solenoid were located in a spot where they could overheat but once they had cooled down they would work just fine.

I figured, "Another twenty minutes and we should be good to go." Everyone exited the van so we all just hung out. Over the years we'd had Flattery she had never failed to start after resting for up to 45 minutes. Twenty minutes later we climbed back in the van. I was so confident she would start that I didn't even test her before I loaded up the kids.

Anyway, I reached down and turned the key and again, nothing happened. "Another twenty minutes!" one of the kids shouted. So again, everyone got out of the van. Twenty minutes later it was beginning to get dark and I was starting to get worried. Parents were expecting us in about an hour and it was an hour's drive from the top of the grapevine into East Los Angeles.

So we all sat down in the van again. I reached down and turned the key and yet again, no response! Jacob, who was one of the older kids, was sitting in the back seat. He said, "John, we should pray for the van to start." I turned to see some smiling faces and nodding heads. "Jacob, that is a good idea. You pray for the van."

Jacob rejoined, "John, I can't pray. I've never prayed before out loud in public." I responded, "Don't worry about it. You are just making the choice to talk to God. That is a good choice. He wants us to talk to Him so just tell Him what is going on and ask Him to help us."

It was amazing to watch Jacob get himself ready for his first public prayer. He started by sitting up straight, running his fingers through his hair, and straightening his shirt. He had been around us for a couple of years so he had observed a pattern to follow should he want to.

Jacob declared, "All right, everyone, fold your hands and bow your heads." He looked around to make sure everyone was in the correct posture then said, "Dear God, the van is broke, and we need to get home, and You can fix it, so fix it. Amen."

I was finding it hard to sit still in the front seat. I was watching one of our kids bloom right in front of my eyes. I may have preferred a little more "ask" and not quite as much "tell" in the prayer, but Jacob was talking to God and I loved it.

I said, "All right, here we go." We had been sitting in the cool of the evening on top of a mountain for over an hour. Flattery had never failed to start in that amount of time on a hot day in a hot place. I just knew that she was going to start and that with Jacob's prayer God was going to get all the credit.

This is the kind of teaching moment everyone who works with kids dreams about. Whether you are a parent, teacher, youth minister, a Sunday school teacher, it doesn't matter. This opportunity is as good as it gets.

I reached down and turned the key. Nothing happened.

In less than half a second I went from completely elated to totally frustrated. I had been pumped up with adrenalin and the next instant I crashed into despair. "God, what are You doing?!" I thought. "Here we are in a desolate place and we really needed Your help and one of Your kids prayed the perfect prayer to set You up for Your big moment and You missed Your cue! Are you asleep up there? Are You paying attention? I've been working with these kids day after day for years to get them to this perfect time and place. What is going on?"

Then from the back seat Jacob said, "John, I know why Flattery didn't start." After taking a few moments to get myself under control and rebound from my mental temper tantrum I inquired, "Jacob, please tell me what you mean. Why do you think she didn't start?" His answer was direct: "I didn't really believe talking to God would do any good."

Out of the blue a clear sense of peace came over me. I turned around again and started explaining who God is and how prayer works, that if we choose to talk to God He is always willing to hear us. I went on to say that if what we want is what He wants He makes it happen—but that He is not like Santa Claus. I reflected, "You can't ask for anything and then demand Him to do for you what you should be doing for yourself."

Then I said, "Jacob, I choose you to pray again. You did well before. We just need to believe that God cares about us and is willing to help us because we do need His help right now to get the van started so we can all get home on time."

"All right," Jacob said. He announced, "Everyone, we are going to pray again, and I want everyone to pray with me and we are all going to believe this time. So now, everyone, fold your hands and bow your heads."

Jacob prayed, "Dear God, the van is broke, and we need to get home, and You can fix it, so fix it. Amen."

Now I was really scared. What would I do if the van didn't start? In that moment of stretching faith I took whatever confidence I could muster, reached down, and turned the key. The van roared to life. Everyone cheered. We began the drive home.

On the road the kids talked about what had happened. Sheryl directed much of the conversation. She taught about understanding the power of God and that it was not right to try to scam Him or take advantage of Him. Me? I was just basking in the glow of watching God work in these kids' lives and in ours.

Somewhere during the next hour the group started calling Flattery, "God's Van." I'm not really sure who said it first but the name stuck. From then on that is what we called her.

But that is not the end of the story. For the next two years until we traded it in on a bigger van we never experienced another mechanical problem with God's Van. I would love to tell you that God permanently fixed the problem. I don't know. But I do know this: Flattery was a temperamental old rust bucket going to Yosemite but on the way home she was transformed into "God's Van." Led by Jacob, our kids prayed, watched, and experienced a supernatural event.

Jacob still lives in Los Angeles. He and I still talk once in a while and, I am happy to report, he continues to talk to God.

David

Sheryl walked in the side door of the Community Center one day and knew something was wrong. It just didn't smell right. Fumes were present but they weren't smoke. There was no odor of a sewer leak, but something wasn't right. As she walked up the stairs she started seeing things out of place. That wasn't unusual after all, we worked with kids. As she climbed the stairs she heard voices from the upstairs playroom. As she reached the top of the stairs she saw powder everywhere. It looked like someone had exploded a baby powder bomb.

Her curiosity took over. Hearing voices and observing powder — what was going on? She had to round a couple of corners but eventually she came face to face with four of our boys. These ten- to twelve-year olds were sitting around a table eating frozen brownies. Sheryl stood there in her most intimidating posture with her hands on her hips and just stared at them until they noticed her and said, "What?!"

Sheryl questioned them, "Yeah, what are you doing here?"

"We were up on the roof and found a way in through the

bell tower so we decided to come in."

"Where did you get the brownies?"

"They were in the freezer."

"How long have you been in here?"

"Oh—about a couple hours."

Sheryl was determined. "Okay, this is what you are going to do. Each of you is going to take a piece of paper and write down how you got in, who did what, who said what, and everything you have done since you have been in here today."

As they started writing, she called 911. When they were done writing she had them sign their papers and date them. About that time five police cars showed up. In our neighborhood when the police show up so do your neighbors. You have to get your entertainment in whatever way you can.

The police walked upstairs and Sheryl took them into the kitchen to talk to the kids. One of them asked, "What is going on?"

Sheryl told the police, "Those four boys broke through

the bell tower in the roof and had been making themselves at home here for the past couple of hours."

The policeman questioned Sheryl, "What did they do?"

Sheryl replied, "All I know so far is that they have been eating our brownies."

The policeman answered, "I'm not sure what we can do to them because they are minors. We can't even question them without parent approval. All they have to say is that they found the hole in the roof and they were just investigating."

At that point Sheryl handed the policemen the signed and dated papers and asked, "Will these help?" The policeman read for a few minutes and found out who broke the wooden slats, who took the brownies out of the freezer, and which of the boys had set off the fire extinguishers (the source of the powder).

Referring to the documents the cop inquired, "Where did these come from?"

"I had them write what they did."

"And they did it? And they signed them?"

The handcuffs came out. The boys were detained and led

down to the police cars. At that point one mother came to Sheryl and said, "What are you doing to David?"

"I'm not doing anything. The police are arresting them for breaking and entering, theft, and vandalism."

"Why are you doing this to my son?"

Sheryl stated, "I'm not doing anything. This is what happens when a person makes these kinds of choices."

From the distraught mom, "But you could tell the police to forget the whole thing. You could stop this."

Sheryl was firm. "Yeah, I suppose I could, but what lesson would David and his friends learn from this experience if I did that?"

From the even more distraught mom, "I don't care. I don't want the police to take David away."

Our relationship with David's mother did not improve after this incident even though we allowed David to come back to the Community Center a couple of months later. At that time he apologized for causing so many problems but eventually we had to expel him. As a result of the original incident he had only been in juvenile court for about three hours and then had been released into the care of his parents.

He hadn't learned his lesson. He continued to make poor choices.

There was one positive result: he never broke into the facility again. We reinforced the bell tower and eventually replaced the original roof with a metal one to make any temptation to enter illegally a little harder to yield to. But it was too late for David.

Prior to being caught breaking and entering our facility he already had experienced a ride or two in a police car. His problems remained. Even though he had been exposed to the juvenile justice system he hadn't learned that bad choices bring negative consequences. What he had learned and believed was that you seldom get caught anyway and even if you do, your mother will be there to bail you out.

David is now in jail and has been incarcerated most of his adult life. He has been convicted of two felonies. If he is convicted of one more, according to current California law, he will be in jail for the rest of his life.

Life *is* full of choices.

Joe

Joe had visited the Community Center occasionally. The first time I connected with him and his siblings was the day when they all came to the Community Center hungry. Joe introduced his brothers and sisters to me. I was impressed with their ability to shake hands and engage in a decent conversation.

A few minutes after finishing his after school snack Joe's older brother Ramon, age eleven, asked if he could have some more. I said, "No, the rule is that everyone can have one serving and besides we will be going outside for recreation in a few minutes."

Ramon said, "Okay, but I sure am hungry."

I inquired, "What did you eat for lunch?"

"Nothing."

"What did you eat for breakfast?"

"Nothing."

"What did you eat last night?"

"Nothing."

I was shocked. I directed, "Okay. Get ready to go outside."

We had learned a lot by working with kids in East LA.

These young kids possessed advanced degrees in stretching the truth, bending it into something that worked for them whenever they wanted, and they had been doing it since preschool. I needed verification before I acted on what I had heard. I went to Ramon's younger sister and said, "Paula, what did you eat for dinner last night?"

"Nothing."

"What about breakfast this morning?"

"Nothing."

"Aren't you hungry?"

"Yes."

Now I had something more concrete to think about, but I still knew I was working with kids who were adept at playing the game. "Okay," I said, "we'll be going outside in a few minutes." Across the room I saw Joe, the family member I knew best. At age nine he was the second oldest sibling. I headed his way.

I inquired, "Joe, what did you eat for lunch?"

Joe replied, "I didn't have time for lunch today because I was reading in the library."

"Okay, what did you eat for dinner last night?"

"Uh, I didn't eat dinner last night."

"Joe, where is your mom?"

"She left yesterday. I'm sure she will be back tonight or tomorrow."

I questioned, "Does she leave you with food and stuff when she leaves?"

His answer was revealing. "No, usually she just locks the door when she needs to get away and we just wait on the stairs until she comes back."

I had heard more than enough. I got Sheryl's attention and told her that when everyone went outside for recreation I wanted Joe and the siblings to stay there in the kitchen. I was going down stairs to our Food Bank Room and find something for them to eat. I don't even remember what I found. It was probably some noodles or soup or something like that—nutrition in a can—easy to open, heat, and serve.

We took care of their hunger and we cared for them. We found a place in the neighborhood for these kids where they could spend the night, and we worked with the authorities for the next three years as they worked with the family to improve their environment. Eventually the six kids were sent to live with relatives.

I wish I could tell you that everything turned out fine. I can't do that. Of the six kids, three have spent most of their lives in jail. These three haven't wanted to maintain much contact with us over the years. I can only hope they have learned that their poor choices have worked against them and prevented them from enjoying a better and more productive life.

The other three kids have done well. They graduated from High School. Joe finished college. He is married, has two children of his own, and lives in Florida. His next younger sister, Paula, is still in college in Washington. The youngest of the six just finished High School. I understand that she accepted a full scholarship to Yale and will be starting college in the fall of 2011.

I visited with Joe in 2010. During our conversation we talked about "Life Is Full of Choices." He said, "Tell everyone my story. Tell them that when I was a kid I hated it every time you said, 'Life is full of choices,' but now I know that it was exactly what I needed. I wouldn't be where I am now if I hadn't realized the importance of my choices."

Then he added something I will always treasure. "My kids hear the phrase 'Life is full of choices' every day."

Conclusion and Acknowledgements

This book lays the foundation for understanding Life Is Full of Choices. It shows how using the Three Cornerstones and the Four Core Needs can meet the central needs of kids and provide power, responsibility, and freedom in their lives.

Children are a precious resource. They need to know how to differentiate between the qualities of life and the circumstances of life. They must learn and activate the internal resources necessary to make better choices, in order to focus their energies on the more important of the two.

The Three Cornerstones help point children in the right directions in order for them to develop into emotionally healthy adults. The cornerstones compose positive environments for growing kids and are used as tools of encouragement.

The Four Core Needs help us understand and relate to our kids. They help us recognize why our kids act like they do. They illustrate the requirement for consistency in our words and actions.

Cornerstones and Core Needs of Growing Kids is the first book within the *Life Is Full of Choices Series*. Its companion book, *Parenting From the Top of the Mountain* shows how to take the principles of the cornerstones and core needs and apply them to the job of parenting. The third book, *Seven Steps to the Top of the Mountain* takes those principles and lays out a road map of practical application in real life.

Cornerstones and Core Needs of Growing Kids tells our story. It teaches the lessons we learned from the kids we served but this book wouldn't have been possible without other people's help.

It is said, "No one writes a book by themselves." I have come to believe this is true. All the people who have helped from Creative Team Publishing deserve a huge thank you. This book would not be in your hands without the work of Glen Aubrey, Heather Hoffman, Jeff Goble, Jordan Trementozzi, and Justin Aubrey.

There were many people who helped us along the way. I want to acknowledge the missionary staff we worked with.

They helped us create and implement these ideas. I also want to thank the hundreds of volunteers who experimented with us in our efforts to find effective ways of affecting kid's lives.

Hundreds of people have supported us in prayer and through financial giving for over 30 years. We offer thanks to those who have contributed to our support through World Gospel Mission, City Team Ministries, Cru (formerly Campus Crusade for Christ), and most recently through Life Is Full of Choices. Their prayers were powerful and helped us through the times when some questioned what we were doing in Los Angeles.

Several individuals have been especially gracious at key moments in our ministry. For being there when we needed them I would like to extend a special thank you to the people of East Whittier Friends Church in Whittier, California, Harmony Evangelical Church in Portland, Oregon, and to Rodger and Mary Aday, Jenny Cosand, Corey and Sharla Gottschalk, David and Sharon Lang, and Mert and Betty Lawson. The choices they made might not have seemed like a big deal at the time, but the effect on us was huge.

A very special word of appreciation goes to both of my mothers and fathers. One set came with my birth, the other one I chose when I married Sheryl. This book would never have been possible without their love for us and their prayers over us.

Thank you to our kids, Brian and Paul, who have spent their lives training me in the skills necessary to be their father. Brian has left childhood behind and become a man who is making good choices about where he lives and how he "does life." Paul and his wife, Katie, are hard at work raising our two grandsons, Liam and David. It is fun watching them parent two very active kids and hear them talk about choices. Paul and Katie also gave me the idea of turning the book about our ministry and the discovery of the Three Cornerstones and the Four Core Needs into this series. That was a great idea. Katie worked with me designing our logo. If you ever saw the original Life Is Full of Choices logo I had designed, you would know why I appreciate her talent and effort so much!

I am so proud of our kids. They have not settled for lives driven by circumstantial whims; instead, they have chosen to use enduring qualities as their targets and measurements. They have chosen well and are thriving.

Finally, marrying Sheryl was the second best choice I ever made. I can hear the questions about "second best choice." The answer: developing a relationship with Jesus was the best choice.

Sheryl has helped me develop as a man, husband, father, and now as a proud grandfather. I could not imagine life without her. This book would never have been possible without her help and encouragement. Thank you, Sheryl.

Life Is Full of Choices
www.LifeIsFullOfChoices.org

life is full of choices

What We Believe:

Life Is Full of Choices is an organization that believes people have the power to choose the qualities of their life. When people choose their qualities they determine who they are and how they will be perceived by those around them. We believe qualities of life are more important than any circumstances.

What We Do:

We teach adults how to work with kids. Adults create lasting impressions on these young lives as they pass important qualities from one generation to the next. We show them effective methods of training kids to make better choices.

We also teach kids. It's fun, challenging, exhausting, and rewarding. We learn from them as we teach them. In fact, they are some of our greatest instructors.

Why We Do It:

Remember, it's about the kids. We have the responsibility to train them about choices, consequences, empowerment, responsibility, and freedom. Join us as we help kids today and positively affect lives for their generation and many to come.

John and Sheryl Emra
Are Available To Speak
To Your Group

Please visit www.LifeIsFullOfChoices.org.
Contact them about scheduling a Life Is Full of Choices
event for your church or with your group.
schedule@LifeIsFullOfChoices.org

For individual mentoring:
mentoring@LifeIsFullOfChoices.org

Contact John and Sheryl Emra by phone.

(855) AT LIFOC or (855) 285-4362

Purchase "choice" products at
www.LifeIsFullOfChoices.com.

CPSIA information can be obtained at www.ICGtesting.com
Printed in the USA
BVOW072255311012

304390BV00002B/2/P

9 780983 891901